W9-DBF-024

C. IE

Melvin Johnson
2/20/68

THE CHRISTIAN FUNERAL

Books by EDGAR N. JACKSON

This Is My Faith
How to Preach to People's Needs
Understanding Grief
A Psychology for Preaching
You and Your Grief
Facing Ourselves
The Pastor and His People
For the Living
Telling a Child About Death
The Christian Funeral

THE
CHRISTIAN
FUNERAL

Its Meaning, Its Purpose,
and Its Modern Practice

EDGAR N. JACKSON

Channel Press   New York

Copyright © 1966 by Edgar N. Jackson

*All rights reserved. No part of this
book in excess of five hundred words may
be reproduced in any form without
permission in writing from the publisher.
First edition.*

CHANNEL PRESS
AFFILIATE OF
MEREDITH PRESS

*Library of Congress Catalog Card
Number: 66-25968
Manufactured in the United States of
America for Meredith Press*

ACKNOWLEDGMENTS

The author acknowledges with gratitude the following permissions to quote from previously published material:

From "The Bridge Builder" by Will Allen Dromgoole in *Masterpieces of Religious Verse*, edited by James Dalton Morrison. By permission of Harper & Row, Publishers.

From "The Way" by John Oxenham in *Masterpieces of Religious Verse*, edited by James Dalton Morrison. By permission of Harper & Row, Publishers.

From "Heir and Serf" by Don Marquis. Copyright 1919 by The Sun Printing and Publishing Co., Inc. From the book, *Poems and Portraits*, by Don Marquis. Reprinted by permission of Doubleday & Company, Inc.

From "The Awakening" by Don Marquis. Copyright 1920 by The Sun Printing and Publishing Co., Inc. From the book, *Poems and Portraits*, by Don Marquis. Reprinted by permission of Doubleday & Company, Inc.

From "The Via Dolorosa" by Edgar N. Jackson. Copyright 1956 Christian Century Foundation. Reprinted by permission from the March 1956 issue of *The Pulpit*.

From *The Living and the Dead* by W. Lloyd Warner. By permission of Yale University Press, Publisher.

From *Death, Grief and Mourning* by Geoffrey Gorer. Copyright © 1965 by Geoffrey Gorer. Reprinted by permission of Doubleday & Company, Inc.

CONTENTS

PART I

THE SIGNIFICANCE
OF THE CHRISTIAN
FUNERAL

In the midst of life there is death. Among those over-whelmed by the fact of death, there is a concern for life and its meaning. Out of the Christian's concern for the "abundant" life and the fact of tragic death—yes, even the death upon the cross—there grows a body of thought and practice that tries to cope with death wisely and well. By meeting death wisely and well, we mean not to be stampeded into foolishness or extravagant activity on the one hand, or retreating into denials and deprivations on the other. Rather with a full recognition of the needs of body, mind, and spirit we would employ with wisdom the full resources of the Christian community in order to emerge, strengthened and sustained by "an unfaltering trust" that there is more to life than death as a goal and more to grief than blind and meaningless suffering. From these affirmative hopes grow a body of practices and attitudes that we would now explore.

The funeral service, a final communal act to recognize the unique value of a specific person, has had a long and illuminating history in Christendom. It grows out of a group of profound and powerful emotions, like love, guilt, concern, respect, identification, and self-preservation. When we examine those funeral arrangements that were made and recounted in the Gospels at the time of the death of our Lord, we get a glimpse of what must have been a standard practice at that time. The body was treated with respect and placed in a special spot reserved for the bodies of the dead. Those who were close to the dead person in life continued their closeness through the ministrations made in death. This included the ceremonial events, the ritualized preparation of the body for entombment. Various members of the family and circle of close friends made their visits to the sepulcher to fulfill their own awareness of obligation, realizing the necessity to fulfill these obligations to the best of their ability.

The nature of the early church made it necessary that its life be centered about small-group activities. Persecution dictated that. Yet the activities of the small groups did not neglect the concern for wise living and a dignified treatment of the dead. The private burying places with their hidden underground chapels attest at least one of the purposes of the catacombs.

When the church became an accepted institution, this dual ministration to the living and the dead was continued through the use of places of worship as places for entombment. The cathedrals of Europe and England were also the resting places of the bodies of the faithful in death. When space requirements made the church buildings inadequate, the bodies of the faithful were interred as near to the sanctuary as possible, and often the churchyard became also the cemetery. (This practice still prevails in many communities.) Even there, when the space was limited, the church procured land on the edge of town and consecrated for its special use the cemetery as a place of burial.

There has always been a visible concern of the church for its members who have died, but even greater has been its concern for the emotion of the living members who continued to live with the feelings of grief and the painful processes of mourning. To them the church spoke directly of a faith that was not overwhelmed by death.

What has been a traditional interest of the church for its members has now become a new focus for study. With the renewed interest in pastoral care the church has made a concentrated effort to meet the specific needs of its people in the face of the crises of life.

The Modern Dilemma

One of the interesting things that is developing in the current attitude toward funeral practices is the deviation from normally accepted procedures in regard to research and scientific study. It would appear that powerful emotional forces are at work to discount or disregard the usual respect for objective study that characterizes most areas of our organized life.

At a time when practically all of the competent and objective research is going in one direction, the recommendations in regard to reforms in funeral practice appear to discount or ignore these findings and go their separate way with a heavy charge of emotion and a breakdown of objectivity.

There are at least four reasons for this apparent failure of those interested in the nature and practice of funeral customs to show cognizance of the significant and serious study going on in the personality sciences to illuminate the matter of death and our ways of coping with it.

First is the subtle and pervasive intrusion of secular values into the individual and group behavior of our culture. If one looks carefully at the criticisms that are raised concerning modern funeral practice, it is apparent that the matter of cost is the prevalent point of evaluation. Monetary considerations tend to be used as the point of judgment as to what is good and what is not good. The leaders of movements toward reform write and speak as if the good funeral is inexpensive and the bad one is marked by extravagant expenditure. This becomes quite obviously an inadequate base for determining the meanings and purposes of socially significant rites and rituals. But such secular judgments are quite characteristic of our culture.

Second, we have the contrasting judgment of those who provide services to families at time of death. The funeral director has in many instances followed the lead of churches and other social institutions in providing sumptuous accommodations, with wall-to-wall carpeting, pleasing decor, parking facilities, and the other evidences of an affluent society. The nature of his vested interests, privately provided as a service to the community, puts the funeral director in a vulnerable spot in objectively judging the criticisms directed toward him. His attitude is that he must serve the needs of the community when death comes whatever the circumstances of those who call upon him. But he may quite naturally feel that he should not be taken advantage of by those who call upon him in time of crisis for services they are unwilling or unable to pay for. Here, again, such secular judgments fall short of what would be desired in establishing the personal and social significance of ceremonies, rites, and ritualized group behavior.

Third is the prevalent antimortal philosophy by which man looks at himself. His dependence upon technology and his faith in science and its ability to solve all problems move him away from his contemplation of himself as a mortal being. So he tends to look at death and all that surrounds it as illusory, unreal, and not to be taken seriously. Large segments of the population are so "scared to death of death" as a fact of human existence and man's mortal nature that they even resent those persons, funeral directors and clergymen, who are the living symbols of man's need to accept his true nature. Only when he can accept himself as a mortal being can he face his moral and social responsibility. When he denies his mortality he tends to build a philosophy of escape, living more and more for the day and less and less for life in its wholeness. This destroys his perspective and leads him to think of death as a disease merely awaiting an adequate cure. Doctors admit thinking of death as essentially an accident, not meant to happen. They even speak of cardial accidents, cerebral accidents, circulatory accidents, and a whole variety of organic events that do not so much signal the breakdown of a mortal organism as an evidence of failure to live wisely and well. The lengthening of the life span so dramatically in recent decades only tends to fortify this attitude of mind, so that man lives more and more in a death-denying, death-defying state. This attitude ill suits him for contemplating life with an adequate philosophy that is related to both life and death. In fact, it further fortifies his escape from reality. So, increasingly, real death becomes a tabooed subject, like sex a few generations ago. Serious consideration of the end of life is avoided as any serious discussion of the beginnings of it were in the recent past.

Fourth is the remoteness of objective scientific inquiry

from the prevalent emotions. The scientist and researcher works at his task in order to find facts. He is not, generally speaking, precommitted to a conclusion. He is interested in finding out what is happening so that he can proceed toward conclusions on the basis of his findings. When what he finds is contrary to the prevalent mood, his finding may very well be rejected, and he may be rejected along with it. The history of science is replete with those instances where facts assaulted fancy, and for the time being at least, fancy held the field. One need only mention Galileo, Bruno, Darwin, Semmelweis, Curie, and Freud to recall this emotional assault on scientific truth, even by scientists. So Herman Feifel, who has pioneered in studies on the modern meaning of death, comments that he was ill prepared to face the opposition to his findings that once assailed Ignaz Semmelweis. The strong emotions of a death-denying, death-defying culture have in practice prevented the findings of the careful researcher from general consideration, and have lifted up the hysterical and the disturbed to places of prominence they little merit, only because their emotions more readily fit the mood of those who give them status.

In the face of these four considerations it is important for us, nevertheless, to look carefully at what the serious students of personality have been discovering about our prevalent attitudes toward death and to see if we can find out what these things mean. Then on the basis of that meaning we may be able to look more wisely at those individual and group practices in which we engage at the time of death to see how well they serve those purposes that are compatible with our Christian faith.

NEW LIGHT ON OLD WAYS OF DOING THINGS

Interestingly enough, the major research in recent years has not been done by those who traditionally share responsibility for the events at the end of life. Apart from the two important books by Paul Irion, *The Funeral and the Mourners* (Abingdon Press, 1954) and *The Funeral: Vestige of Value* (1966), nothing of significance in this field has been produced by clergymen. Similarly, except for sponsoring some useful historical studies, funeral directors have produced little of significance for understanding the deeper meaning of the rites, rituals, and ceremonials at the end of life.

For our insights, then, we will have to turn to those who work in the behavioral sciences—anthropology, psychology, sociology, and psychosomatic medicine.

Anthropology

William Gladstone, the astute English statesman, once said, "Show me the manner in which a nation or a community cares for its dead, and I will measure with mathe-

9

matical exactness the character of its people, their respect for laws of the land, and their loyalty to high ideals." While he could hardly qualify as an anthropologist, his comment has verifications in the findings of those who study the group practices of mankind, primitive and modern. The attitude toward death, and the type of practices at the time of death are significant projections of group life. Like the old question of chicken and egg, there is difficulty in telling which is cause and which is effect. But certainly there is a demonstrable relationship.

Studies of American Indians done by Erik Erikson and Ruth Benedict, of primitive tribes by Frazer and Malinowski, and of contemporary cultures by Gorer and Mead underline the importance of group ways of doing things for personal and social health. The rites and rituals become group ways of doing things that meet the needs of the total personality—conscious, preconscious, and unconscious. This becomes especially true when the rites and rituals relate to highly emotional events where the deep reservoirs of feelings are channeled into healthful expression.

Perhaps most useful in our present consideration is the recent study by Geoffrey Gorer, an English anthropologist, entitled *Death, Grief, and Mourning* (Doubleday, 1965). He makes a careful study of trends in group behavior and tries to estimate the meaning and effect of these trends on group life. He finds that 44 percent of parents in England say nothing to their children about a death that occurs in the family. When children are excluded from meaningful communication about important emotional events in family life, a vacuum is created that is soon filled by anxiety. This anxiety tends to be cumulative as one generation piles on another its unresolved fears.

Gorer further points out that when a highly emotional event is worked through with a generous supply of time-limited group activity, the anxiety is lessened. When efforts are made to deny the event and the feelings by a minimum of group activity, the anxiety is compounded and tends to plague life for longer periods of time. He says that the times of most acute emotional need among humans are in infancy and when death occurs. He finds that when clergymen give understanding and support at such times, their parishioners respond with appreciation and more rapid psychological movement. When their clergy deny this support and ignore these feelings, resentment builds up and is maintained for long periods of time. He finds that as the expression of grief increases, so also, "With nearly all the others in this group, I had the feeling that, by denying expression of their grief, they had reduced their lives to triviality. . . ." (page 75)

Gorer's conclusions are important for our purpose. He writes:

I think the material presented has adequately demonstrated that the majority of British people are today without adequate guidance as to how to treat death and bereavement, and without social help in living through and coming to terms with the grief and mourning which are the inevitable responses in human beings to the death of someone whom they have loved. The minority who are convinced adherents of religious creeds or sects have the assistance and comfort provided by the traditions and eschatology of their religions and by the social ritual which is interwoven with the religious practices. . . . I think my material illustrates the hypothesis that this lack of accepted ritual and guidance is accompanied by a very considerable amount of maladaptive behavior, from the triviality of meaningless "busyness" through the private rituals of what I have called mummification to the apathy of despair. To the best of my knowledge, there is no analogue from either the records of past societies or the description of present societies outside the Judeo-Christian tradition to this situation in which the majority of the population lacks common patterns or rituals to deal with the crises inherent in man's biological nature. (pages 125-7)

Then, after a discussion of the meaning of the crisis and the need for social readjustment to it, he says:

If these adjustments are not made, the outcome is liable to be either the permanent despair of depression or melancholia, an impairment of the capacity to love in the future, or various irrational attitudes toward death and destruction. . . . If one can deny one's own grief, how much more easily can one deny the grief of others; the one possible outcome of the public denial of mourning is a great increase in public callousness. . . . The "pornography of death," whether it be furtively enjoyed or self-righteously condemned, manifests an irrational attitude toward death and a denial of mourning. . . . The connection between vandalism and the denial of mourning is not quite so direct as is the connection with callousness or irrational preoccupation with, or fear of, death, for it takes into consideration an aspect of mourning which is given no overt expression in our culture. This aspect is the anger felt against the dead for abandoning the survivors. . . . According to some psychoanalysts this anger is a component of all mourning; and one of the main functions of the mourning process is to "work through" and dissipate this anger in a symbolic and, to a great extent, unconscious fashion . . . if this anger is not worked through in mourning, it will turn in on itself and result in the self-reproach and self-punishment which are the most marked symptoms of melancholia . . . it would seem correct to state that a society which denies mourning and gives no ritual support to mourners is thereby producing maladaptive and neurotic responses in a number of its citizens. The period of intense mourning probably varies with the temperament of the mourner and the nature of the relationship with the deceased. My impression is that the median range is between six and twelve weeks. During this period the mourner is in more need of social support and assistance than at any time since infancy and early childhood; and at this moment our society is signally failing to give this support and assistance. The cost of this failure in misery, loneliness, despair and maladaptive behavior is very high. (pages 132-4)

It is well to consider that the foregoing words are the objective evaluation of a social scientist about the state of affairs as he finds them. The conclusions he expresses are an expression of concern we cannot easily ignore.

Sociology

The sociologist stands off to view the organized life of man to see the meaning of his behavior. An earlier generation of sociologists spent most of their time compiling and interpreting statistics about man and his institutions and forms of group behavior. More recently sociologists have increased their concern about what happens to people, their feelings, their values, and their goals in the complex fabric of social life. These younger sociologists, or social psychologists as they might more properly be designated, have undertaken studies to understand the meaning of man's institutions as they relate to aging and death.

These younger sociologists, aware of the increased life span of our generation, of the predominantly youthful makeup of our society (by 1970 over 50 percent will be 25 or under), and the values created by this large group, perceive the rapid movement of people who are separated from their social roots. They also see the breakup of those patterns of behavior that were once significant ways of meeting the emotional crises of life. In our country, which has been both a melting pot of people and a melding place of cultures, the uncertainty about roots among the second and third generations of newly arrived families was already a problem. Now with widespread migrations of people there are changes that magnify the problem. The nature of family and group cohesiveness is modified. The multigeneration family of a century ago in rural settings has decreased in number as the small-sized family unit has replaced it. This has led to a culture whose values are intensified in a family unit rather than diffused through a generation. Thus the focus of strong emotional investment is reduced and the nature of acute loss is increased when death comes. Instead of a group into which people marry and are born and from which they die, the family has become a unit created by marriage and ended by death. This also seriously affects the process of handing down those ways of doing things that are significant because of their ability to meet unconscious and subconscious emotional needs. When nothing happens to replace these modes of significant behavior, people are left with blank spots in behavior, and these ultimately become blank spots in values, as Gorer has shown.

In an important book, *Death and Identity* (Wiley, 1965), Robert Fulton has brought together the writings of a number of persons who have been exploring the social meaning of attitudes toward death in our culture. Here it is pointed out that funeral rites serve three purposes: properly to dispose of a dead body, to aid the bereaved to reorient themselves from the shock of death, and to publicly acknowledge and commemorate a death while asserting the viability of the group. Doing things in proper order with well-recognized and generally accepted ceremony "reminds one that there is structure and order in the social system." The funeral is a "rite of passage." As such it not only marks the completion of a life but also "reaffirms the social character of human existence." The funeral then is a form of group protection, in the face of individual death, to affirm the values of life and the community, and direct future living toward these values.

> The denial of death and the deritualization of mourning growing apace in America today parallel and reflect other significant changes apparent in family life. These changes can be identified briefly as: 1) from predominance of the religious to predominance of the secular, 2) from a large group to a small group, 3) from a stable to a mobile group, 4) from an adult-centered to a child-centered family, 5) from a communal family ideology to a democratic one, 6) from an integrated to an individualized group, and 7) from a neighborhood-enclosed family to an isolated family in an urban environment. (page 335)

Fulton points out that about half of the people in the United States no longer have an active affiliation with a church, an institution that tends to give stability to ritualized practice in the community. He further points out that the waning role of the clergy, and especially the Protestant minister, is compounded by a lack of awareness of the personal and social significance of ceremonials. In fact, in some instances the clergy even seem to support the movements that would hasten the process of removing significant ceremonials and rituals at the "rites of passage," because they are unaware of their role as pastors and of the subconscious purposes of group rituals. This tends to give to death a more and more impersonal and unimportant quality that, in turn, tends to make life itself more impersonal and unimportant.

If death is increasingly considered to be a disease or an accident, the question is raised as to the real meaning of life. If man is a mortal creature, his life and his death are important aspects of his personal history. His death cannot be treated as meaningless without bringing to all of life the threat of meaninglessness. The Nazi experiment with values showed that life is indivisible and that, when any persons or groups are treated with disdain, all values suffer in consequence. What was learned by cruel history is reaffirmed in the ways people use to express, in ritualized form, the meaning they attribute to life and the values they invest in the community. So it is that Lloyd Warner arrives at his estimate of the significance of the local cemetery in the small New England town:

> As long as the cemetery is being filled with a fresh stream of the recently dead, it stays symbolically a live and vital emblem, telling the living of the meaning of life and death. . . . The symbols of death say what life is and those of life define what death must be. The meanings of man's fate are forever what he makes them. (pages 380-1) *

Many of the changes that the sociologist records are not the product of plan or design. They are the unexamined concomitants of social and cultural change. But when we sense destructive meanings that are a byproduct of the

* *The Living and the Dead,* Yale University Press, 1959.

change, then we are obliged to examine processes, evaluate their meanings, and try to create new and significant attitudes toward social usage that can do for us in the future the important things that old ways of doing things did for those who lived in the past.

Psychology

Psychology, with its deep interest in understanding the mind and emotions of men, is also concerned with the meaning for life of the event of death. In recent years this quest for understanding has pursued the exploration of the lower levels of consciousness. St. Paul stated the problem, and St. Augustine amplified it. It is that men often do what they do not want to do and do not do what they want to do, and they do not understand what is at work within them to produce this apparently contradictory state of affairs. The psychologist finds that major segments of mental activity are not easily subject to what we speak of as conscious or rational mental processes. These major areas of mental activity have great power to influence life and behavior. So it is important to understand them.

The psychologist in studying the attitudes toward death finds that men build defenses against the painful or unpleasant; they feel guilty or angry, and fail to understand the source of their feelings, and try to overcompensate by attributing meanings to those things that are not real, at the same time that they tend to look away from what is actually happening. In a book, *The Meaning of Death* (McGraw-Hill, 1959), Herman Feifel, a clinical psychologist, has gathered together the insights of a number of students of human personality to examine this behavior to see what it means. In literature, in art, and in life men act out their deep feelings. They try to cope with space, time, the meaning of existence, and the awareness of God. Religion seems to be an organized effort to find explanations for the mysteries of life and at the same time project meanings and purposes adequate to sustain the conscious mind in the processes of living.

Dr. Feifel finds a prevalent practice of escape into unreality to avoid looking at life as it is. This effort to escape the inescapable leads to anxiety and the effort to live in a world of make-believe. Specialization tends to remove death from the context of living, so that, while a hundred years ago it was a common experience in households and communities, death is now a remote event, taking place in the presence of emotionally unrelated but technically skilled specialists—physicians, nurses, state police, and military attendants. The effect of this is to deny the reality of the event, for it is remote from experience. Yet, when asked by Dr. Feifel as to their preference as to the circumstances of death, the vast majority of his answerers said they would want to die at home in the presence of those they love. Because conditions change, so also do attitudes. But when we are concerned about important value-creating processes, it is important for us to create the emotional equivalents of what have been removed by circumstance. Feifel concludes:

> We are mistaken to consider death as a purely biologic event. The attitudes concerning it, and its meaning for the individual, can serve as an important organizing principle in determining how he conducts himself in life. (page 123)

Other psychological studies verify this relationship of the attitude toward death to the quality of life. Mervyn Schoor,

M.D., in his study of the deviant behavior of children, supports the earlier study of Rollo May, *The Meaning of Anxiety* (Ronald Press, 1950), in pointing out that the problem of juvenile delinquency may more often be the acting out of the feelings of a grieving child, rather than the simple expression of destructive anger.

Lawrence LeShan, a clinical psychologist, whose depth studies of the cancer patient have won international recognition, points out that the onset of cancer is often related to the loss of meaning for life as well as to the loss of a person dearly loved. Dr. LeShan says that, in his depth studies of cancer patients, he almost invariably finds a state of "bleak and unutterable despair." His theory is that emotions most immediately affect the glandular system, and the glandular system controls body chemistry, and the body chemistry controls disease systems and tends to control abnormal cell division. When a chronically unresolved emotional problem produces a state of persistent body imbalance, the conditions are favorable for the development of neoplastic tissue. So the breakdown of the healthful processes of mourning may well be related to the increased incidence of malignancy in our time.

Many other studies could be mentioned, but these should suffice to show the importance from the psychological point of view of taking a long look at the significance of the ritualized methods we employ, or fail to employ, in working through our grief.

Medicine

Some of the earliest insight and some of the more important findings on the impact of grief upon life have come from those who do psychosomatic research. The basic assumption here is that illness is a form of behavior through which the organism works out its problems in physical form. This necessity usually comes about when the normal expression of emotion has been thwarted and so is repressed or diverted. Then, with time, it shows up in disguised form, sometimes in changed personality traits, sometimes in behavior patterns, but yet at other times in the response of the physical organism in what we call disease.

Lindemann's pioneering study of ulcerative colitis shows how the organism dramatically acts out emotional states. The findings of the Lindemann study showed a high percentage of unwisely managed grief within the period of six months before the onset of the symptoms. What appears to take place is that the organism, unable to let go of the lost love object as the essential act of mourning, becomes involved in a sum-total organic response of holding on to unrelated objects. Even body waste—held on to until it ferments, causing inflammation and tissue breakdown and ulceration—is but a form of acting out the feelings that cannot find normal expression.

Other studies have related physical symptoms to unresolved grief reactions. Sometimes it may be some of the component emotions of grief that assert themselves. In her book, *Emotions and Bodily Changes* (Columbia University Press, 1935), Flanders Dunbar traces certain heart conditions to fear, certain digestive conditions to anger, and upper respiratory disturbances to an inability to cry normally. It is easy to see how conditions such as these could at least in part be explained in some instances by the failure of the person to work through his emotions adequately at the time when they were acutely felt. So the acute that is repressed becomes chronic. The reservoir of the emotions which can be poured out in healthy fashion under some circumstances is blocked under others and tends to produce the state of repressed, regressed, or sublimated emotion. Our concern, then again, becomes the way in which we can help people to express feelings in healthy fashion rather than have them repressed until they manifest themselves in unhealthy manner. Healthy ceremonials provide channels of expression that can make natural feelings acceptable, at the same time that a full facing of reality is encouraged. This facing of reality can be surrounded by traditional expression and living support by the group that is an expression of man's confidence in himself and a trust in the social groups that sustain him in crisis.

It is not strange, then, that Dr. James Knight, Professor of Psychiatry at Tulane Medical School, should state that the major field of psychosomatic research at the present time is the side effects of unwisely managed response to deprivation experiences. Certainly, death is, for most people, the most acute type of deprivation they will encounter.

The studies that have been and are now being made in the behavioral sciences—anthropology, sociology, psychology, and the branch of medicine that deals with behavior—all point up for us the significance of the personal and group responses to death. When these responses are limited, marked by denials, and lead to illusion or repression, the outcome is maladaptation to life and also neurotic behavior. When healthy patterns are employed and the useful ritualized procedures are made available by society to its members, the persons suffering grief are more apt to move through it with wholeness of being and move into the future free from lasting injury from the experience.

VALUES OF HEALTHFUL CEREMONIAL PROCEDURES

One of the basic functions of religious practice is to give meaning to life so important that persons are inspired to achieve the fullest possibilities of life. The ceremonials of the church serve this purpose. Baptism recognizes the sacred partnership with God that exists in the creation of a new person. The act of confirmation recognizes the capacity for self-dedication on the part of the individual who verifies what his parents did at his baptism. A wedding recognizes the importance of the new human relationship in the creating of a home. Each of these ceremonies gives dignity and meaning to life by acts of recognition. The institution lends its tradition and its trained personnel to give status to the events in the lives of its members, for in so doing it enhances the meaning of life itself.

When we come to the end of life, proper recognition of the life of the person who has died seems appropriate. But common sense tells us that it does the dead person no good. Of what use is it to him, who is no longer capable of sensation or the use of bodily function, whose capacity for feeling and thought in the physical sense no longer exists, to have his body embalmed and his remains placed carefully in a casket? It quite obviously serves no purpose for the person who has died. But every group in every culture has found it necessary to perform certain rituals at the time of the death of its members. Why? For one simple reason: They do it for themselves. Because they die a little when anyone else dies, they need to verify the dignity and importance of their living and to help guarantee the practices that will protect them from indignity in death when they are helpless and dependent.

Sometimes we hear persons say they do not care what is done with their bodies when they are dead. But we know that cannot be entirely true, for they certainly would object if it became common practice to dump dead bodies in the street like ordinary rubbish. The dignity of man in life claims a comparable dignity in death, for the sake of those who are still alive, able to feel and experience emotional ties yet unbroken with the dead.

As the psychologists point out for us, the processes of identification are complicated. We learn to feel with others as we identify ourselves with their feelings through our own. Why do you say "Ouch" when someone else hits his thumb? Not because it is your thumb, but because you have learned to feel with him through your own experience of thumb hitting. Love is the most highly developed and all-demanding form of identification with another. It relates life in many ways and at many levels of thought and feeling. When death comes to one deeply loved, it is not possible to tear out by the roots all of the complex forms that identification or love takes. Rather, at its own pace the emotional capital invested in another is withdrawn so that it can be reinvested in life where it can continue to bear fruit.

The series of events which recognize with dignity the multiple relationships that have existed and still, at many levels of being, continue to exist, are designed to make it possible for the progressive withdrawal of identification from the lost love object. Lindemann speaks of it as "freeing one's self from the bondage to the deceased." To avoid or deny the necessity of the process is to show a lack of understanding for the psychological processes involved.

The healthful ceremonial provides the climate for doing what sooner or later has to be done in one way or another. The major task of mourning is one of letting go of the past and its objects of affection. This does not mean a denial of memory, but it means a use of memory that can enrich life, not enslave it. The oft-used illustration of the greedy monkey, who put his hand through the small opening of the bottle and took so large a handful of nuts that he could not get his hand out again, is relevant here. The effort to hold on to a fistful of nuts meant he could not escape. This is too great a price to pay for the loss of one's freedom. The wisely conducted funeral service helps preserve the freedom of the future by creating the atmosphere for wisely letting go of the past. Unwise practice denies that there is anything to let go of, so the person unwittingly enslaves himself by his very denial, for he makes it difficult to cope with the real problem honestly.

One of the significant functions of wise practice is to make clear the relationship of death to the "body image." Each person has a feeling for his own body. It is a complicated and largely unconscious set of feelings. When someone close to us dies, we experience an unconscious threat to our body image; we feel the threat of death but are usually unable to articulate it. We are liberated from the feeling of threat by actually facing the dead body of the other person. We have reinforced for ourselves the consciousness that it is *his* body that is dead, not ours. When we studiously avoid viewing the dead body of another, we are in effect stating our distaste or even anxiety at the process of admitting the reality of the event because we are actively related to it. When we say, "I don't want to see the body of my friend, for I want to remember him as he was," we are quite possibly expressing our anxiety. We know very well that the simple fact is that he is not now the way he was; he has never been dead before. While it is good to remember fine things about a person, it is dangerous to try to keep him alive after he has died by this type of mental process.

Therapists working with those who have had acute reactions to their grief have found that a prevalent symptom is a complete loss of the image of the deceased. This form of blocking out of consciousness of a fact of life prevents normal mourning work. In treatment the therapists may well take the disturbed person to a funeral home to confront real death in viewing a dead body. This act, whether of a known person or not, seems to remove the block against facing the reality of death, and the grief work then begins. Wise folkways of nearly every culture down through history have provided a moment of truth when the living confront the fact of death by viewing the body of the group member now dead. Those who say, "No, I want to remember him as he was," should be led to see the implicit denial of reality in their attitude for the important fact is that he is not the way he was. The change brought by death must be accepted in order wisely to recall the life that was. When in normal funeral practice relatives and friends gather about to pay their respects, the oft-repeated phrase, "Doesn't he look natural," is a clear evidence of identification with the image of the deceased, a facing of real death, and an acceptance of the fact that one who has been known in life is now known in death.

This facing of reality is essential for the ministrations of faith, for our faith is geared to reality, no matter how painful, and it has little relationship to a world of fancy, denial, or illusion. The Christian message speaks to real people of real things. It is not a device of escape.

The understanding of rites and rituals leads to a new understanding of the group need to act out the things that cannot so easily be talked about. Students of human behavior, such as Lawrence Abt in his book *Acting Out,* indicate that those experiences with high emotional content are often beyond the capacity of words for expression, but accepted patterns of group behavior vent the feelings and prevent their denial. The funeral practices, though quite varied in different cultures, serve a common purpose in helping people to express feelings that are so powerful that they may be overwhelming unless alternate methods are developed. So tradition gives people a chance to move beyond words to acts. In the traditional rites at death people find ways that are significant for them to communicate feelings. In attire, attitude, behavior, and group practices, they find ways of expressing strong feelings. We find that this is essentially therapeutic and basically sound.

This does not mean, however, that good taste or generally accepted standards of wise procedure should be abrogated. That is why I have recommended that the casket be closed during the religious services both in church and at the funeral home. The value of the period of visitation, or even of the old-fashioned wake, is that it provides an accepted time, place, and atmosphere for the encounter and also prepares one for the next step in the mourning process, the acceptance of the spiritual resources needed to face the fact that the person now dead will not be seen again in this existence. This gives to the church service a special quality, for, while it does not deny by act or attitude the fact of death, it gives its thought and attention to those qualities that have a right to become central, for they will be the sources of strength in the days ahead.

Dr. William M. Lamers, Jr., a West Coast psychiatrist who has studied the group significance of funerals, says that "the funeral is an organized, purposeful, time-limited, flexible, group-centered response to death." It is a recognized way of meeting a real event in life. It has group significance, because it is something that has happened to the group, and so the group participates. It is, generally speaking, the only individual ceremonial event to which members of the group are not specifically invited, and to which all are welcomed. It is a tragic withholding of the resources of the social and religious group to have no such opportunity for the expression of feelings, or to declare that it is so personal and private that all but the most intimate are excluded. This denies the essential nature and purpose of the ceremonial event.

Socially and psychologically the funeral is something we do for ourselves to insure the values of life and to protect ourselves against the anxiety that comes with their denial. It serves some important but unconscious psychological needs by verifying the feelings of identification and the need for a clear body image of the deceased. It gives a chance to act out the process of letting go by group-accepted, group-recognized rituals. It does these things in a clearly defined series of time-limited events that are purposefully controlled by the group to protect itself and also its bereaved members from permanent emotional injury. In these respects the funeral then serves important, though not often understood, functions.

SPIRITUAL VALUES OF THE CHRISTIAN FUNERAL

In the context of our consideration the funeral is a religious service, conducted under the auspices of the church, which provides its ordained leadership and pastoral care for the purpose. It is designed to give special help to the needs of its people and others in time of emotional crisis. How does it seek to do this?

The Christian message grows from an honest confrontation with death that moves beyond the historical event to the spiritual meaning of the event. It is a bold affirmation of faith in the spiritual nature of life. It is perhaps the most audacious act of faith that has grown from man's capacity for ordered thought, profound conviction, and directed effort. It is the focal point where the possibility of God-consciousness meets the actuality of God's revelation through Jesus, the Christ, who faced death but was not overcome by it.

The Resurrection was the dynamic force that changed the early church. It changed the disciples from a disordered group of frightened men to a fearless band of inspired lead-

29

ers. The message they taught was one the ancient world welcomed, for it was overwhelmed by the finite nature of life with its pain, brutality, and apparent cheapness. The message of the Resurrection was one of powerful faith in the meaning of God-consciousness as the key to indestructibility. It was the answer not only to the problems of man's mortality, but it was also the guarantee of the meaning of life itself. If it deserved to gain an eternal quality, it was deserving of important faith and action in living. The changed behavior of the disciples was the living evidence of what this idea meant to them. It quite obviously changed everything.

But if we look closely at the experience of the disciples, we are confused. We tend to look at such things from the point of view of modern science. This event, so important to the disciples, seems to us to be a source of conflict. The biblical record makes it clear that Jesus was so different after death that relatives, close friends, and old acquaintances did not recognize him. He passed through doors without opening them. He walked for miles along the dusty road without his disciples being aware of his identity. Yet the materialization was strong enough to convince a doubting Thomas. St. Paul, who was close to the original events and preached the Resurrection as basic doctrine, made it clear that he believed there was a physical body and a spiritual body, a human form and a resurrection body. The spiritual nature was the expression in death of the undying quality of being, for if even a portion of man is made in the image of God, it cannot be destroyed, for in its creation it has upon it the marks of the infinite and eternal.

Such an idea is difficult for modern man to accept, because he lives in a time of space flight, biological sophistication, and materialistic preoccupation. His life is largely shut off from the mystery of meaning. But this is only superficially so, for all of life is surrounded by the ultimate of mystery, for the more we know about it, the more mysterious it becomes. Our senses are a mystery. We know little of the complicated electrochemical process by which light waves are transformed in our minds into color, pattern, and meaningful design, but it does not keep us from seeing. We know little of the complicated engineering process by which the vibration of air is transferred through a solid to a liquid and then into meaningful revelation, but this does not keep us from hearing. The greater mystery of the spiritual meaning of man's life and the Christian's ultimate triumph over death is no more of a mystery than those complicated processes that are a part of conception, gestation, birth, and growth. We cannot easily accept the meaning of one without confronting the meaning of the other. Yet our day is strangely uncomfortable with the idea of the Resurrection.

Instead of standing dumb before the mystery of death, the Christian funeral gives the opportunity for bringing to people in its most relevant context the great and audacious affirmations of the faith. It is not a time for denial, not a time to act as if a person had done something inhuman, unpatriotic, or un-American by dying. Rather, it is the time for facing the fact of death at the physical level as the basis for claiming the spiritual inheritance that comes with divine sonship. It is the point where we fall to the ground, to rise again.

So the funeral service is the opportunity for an act of worship that is neither trivial nor trite. It is the point at which philosophical completeness is verified and the sacredness of the life that was and the life that is to be are confirmed. The earthen vessel that was capable of building the values associated with God-consciousness fulfills in death that added dimension of its mysterious and mystical meaning. It is a time for a strong utterance that emerges from the daring faith rather than a quiet and cringing despair before a view of life that is essentially materialistic. Rather it can be the affirmation of a faith that is doubly necessary in a day when so much else in life tends to deny it. It is worship in its true meaning, for it is an act of giving worth and dignity to life. It is doubly unfortunate when the prevalent death-denying and death-defying attitude of mind seems to still the voice of faith at the time when it could speak most vigorously and victoriously of the true meaning of man's spiritual existence.

It is our feeling that the Christian funeral can be the most significant group activity at the time of death, for it honestly faces reality, accepts deep feelings, affirms faith, and challenges life to seek its highest spiritual meaning. It is the time of ultimate relevance for seeking these purposes, and in doing it, it is clearly on sound psychological, social, and spiritual ground.

CONCLUSION

Those of us who have the opportunity to make the Christian funeral an important spiritual experience in the lives of our people repeatedly can be thankful that our faith is geared by its content and its tradition to meet the most desperate conditions of the human plight. We would accept the full opportunity and privilege of this highly specialized act of worship and make it a significant part of the church's total witness to the significance of life's meaning.

In summary let us look at what a Christian funeral should do for those who share in it.

First, it should recognize that what is done is to meet the social, psychological, and spiritual needs of those who are able to participate in it. It is not a service for the dead but a service about the dead and their experience of death. It is a recognition of the religious community that no man is an island and that, when anyone dies, we all die a little. It is a time for the living to face the fact of their mortality, that they for a time live a life measured by space and time. Yet in the midst of the measurable they are never unaware of

33

the timeless and the eternal. This living need is the base upon which the service is built.

Second, the service is aware of the powerful emotions that are at work and tries to fulfill the feelings rather than deny them. The person who is trained as an intellectual tends to meet life crises at the intellectual level. This may mean that feelings are denied. But grief is essentially a feeling, and it is not satisfied by intellectualizations. Faith is made up of belief that is intellectualized, emotion that is expressed through conviction, and action which puts belief and conviction to work. The funeral gives people a chance to do certain ritualized acts that make it possible to work through the convictions that cannot easily be put into words. Then, when this has been fulfilled rather than denied, the sustaining power of spiritual truth can become more valid for the distressed mourners.

Third, the funeral is a time for facing reality rather than for denying it. Death is a part of man's experience. It cannot be ignored or avoided without disrupting moral practice and social responsibility. Even though it is a natural inclination for man to seek the comfortable and avoid the unpleasant, it is not a good enough basis from which to meet life. The Christian faith is geared to even the most distressing aspects of reality, and its message becomes triumphantly relevant only when all of life is accepted without illusion or limitation. The viewing of the body prior to the religious service and the presence of the closed casket at the service are the quiet evidence of death and man's willingness to stand in the presence of it in faith, not in fear, in fact, not in fancy. It gives to the service its quality of uniqueness, for there has never been a service quite like it before, and there will never be another quite like it again.

It is an affirmation of the uniqueness of personality. It would be unfortunate to deny this expression of faith by a retreat into a generalized superficial and impersonal moment of embarrassed defiance to the ultimate fact of man's mortal nature.

Fourth, while it would not deny the fact of the event, neither would it deny the validity of the emotions that attend it. Grief is an honorable emotion. It is the expression of the feeling we have about the value of life. It recognizes the relationships that are now broken in loneliness. It recognizes the love now moved beyond the physical object to its spiritual meaning. These feelings have their important place in life. While the Christian funeral would not play upon these feelings mercilessly, neither would it fail to recognize that the feelings exist and need to find a healthful expression. For we do not decide whether or not we will have the feelings. We have only the choice as to how wisely and well we will manage them. We know from sad experience that denial, repression, and suppression are poor substitutes for the honest recognition and valid expression of our feelings. The funeral should give the climate where it is possible to do this wisely and well.

Fifth, the funeral should give the members of the religious community a chance to give evidence of their emotional and spiritual support of the bereaved. In the time of great emotional need it is important to be able to respond. It is also well to remember that, when the need is greatest, it is often the time when it is the most difficult, and we are inclined to run away. It is the homely child that stands most in need of love. So, also, those who are most sorely distressed and difficult to reach are apt to be the most needful of understanding and support.

Sixth, the Christian funeral should be a time of great affirmation. Our whole tradition states that it is not a time of defeat and despair. It is a time to affirm the faith and, by affirming it in the most distressing circumstances, to strengthen it for all other times of life. It is not a time to stand dumb before the ruthless events so attendant upon our physical natures. Rather it is the time to state and restate in most effective form the faith that undergirds and gives meaning to all of life. Like any other service of worship it invites man to stand before the ultimates of existence and face them, not with anxiety and fear, but with fortitude and faith.

When the Christian funeral is approached in this light, it becomes a time of opportunity, not of dismay. It becomes a time of privileged utterance when the deepest meanings of faith and tradition are made available to people in their time of deepest need.

With that in mind we invite an understanding of the place of the funeral meditation in the service at the end of life and also an examination of the possibility of using the sermon as a channel for educating the parish to a more realistic attitude toward death and man's spiritual nature.

If the church can help its members meet the crises of life with courage and insight, all of life is deepened and enriched in its capacity for sympathy, empathy, and understanding. Then the church and its ministry more adequately meet the needs of those who "walk through the valley of the shadow of death."

PART II

THE FUNERAL MEDITATION

If, as we have tried to point out, the funeral is a unique and significant event in the life of the church and the lives of individuals faced with death, it then seems only reasonable that this service should be no trivial and insignificant event.

Too often in recent years the point has been made that the church is interested in life and that its emphasis should be upon the needs of the living. Some ministers have used this idea to excuse a way of conducting funerals that makes them appear afraid to admit that such things exist; the unwanted specter of death is not only not emphasized, but also treated with as little time, thought, and energy as possible.

To this end many funeral services have been reduced to a brief reading of Scripture and perfunctory prayer, almost as if the Christian faith had nothing to say about the relationship of life to death, or the needs of living people carrying a heavy burden of grief and seeking from their religious faith what they need to carry them through the difficult time.

It is my contention that the significant experience of those who are facing death gives to the pastor one of his more important opportunities to speak to the spiritual needs of his people. For mourners are people, and the service is not an effort to usher an unfortunate creature quickly and easily out of the multiple relationships of his existence, but is rather the time when the church and its official representatives recognize an important change in the status of one of its members and an equally important change in the relationships of others of its communicants.

How can the pastor give to the funeral service he conducts a dignity, a strength, and a significance which indicates that the church cares for its suffering members and the Christian faith has something of great importance to say to their need?

There was a time when funeral orations were accepted practice, and the eloquent preacher used the fear of death to flay the sinners who might escape his verbal assaults at other times but were in effect a captive audience at the death of a member of the family. Such poor taste fortunately has been replaced by a deeper concern for those who suffer grief.

The vacuum that was left by the omission of the funeral oration or funeral sermon was in some instances filled by a prepared eulogy or a funeral meditation. In many instances an empty space remained, and the service was reduced to a common usage that was repeated almost without change when death visited the parish.

This retreat into ritual shares an all too prevalent mood in our culture, which feels struck dumb by death and has little or nothing to say, for it feels that there is little or nothing that is relevant. The helpless mood of materialism creeps into every aspect of life, and it is not strange that it should make itself felt here. The fear of death makes us want to ignore its threat to life, and in consequence we surround it with as little meaning as possible.

However, the Christian message from the beginning has felt that it had something important to say about life and death and the needs of those who wrestle with its presence. To evade or avoid the opportunity to speak to this important human experience is to imply that there is nothing that can be said.

It would seem that the wiser procedure would be to seek to make an utterance of faith compatible with the event and the needs of the people participating in it. The place for the funeral meditation then becomes a significant utterance speaking to a special need at a precise and carefully prepared event in the life of the pastor and the parish.

When arrangements for the religious aspects of the funeral have been almost completely left in the hands of the funeral director, the impression is given that the pastor and the church feel that their part in it is unimportant. It would be unfortunate if the significant role of the pastor, the church, and the Christian faith were to be discounted by an act of default.

How, then, could the service be prepared so that it would more nearly meet the unique opportunity it affords, and yet do so with a sensitivity to modern modes of thought and practice?

Certainly the use of Scripture and prayer are of great importance, for they relate the present to the significant insights of men down through the ages and also direct thought toward the resources of the spirit so vitally needed as one seeks the strength to face a drastically changed future.

Scripture and prayer could well be used to prepare mind

and emotion for the effort of speaking to the need of the hour, in the light of Christian insight and practice. There are few times when the testimony of the Christian faith speaks so directly and powerfully to human need as when man is faced with the clear evidence of his mortal nature.

The main burden of this utterance would consist of a meditation, brief, precisely prepared, and carefully designed to meet special needs that exist. Six or seven minutes would probably be adequate time for this meditation. It need not speak specifically of the person who has died, although it might indirectly use points of reference in the life of the deceased to focus the thought.

The meditation should not seek to stimulate the emotions, although it should not try to evade the fact that grief is an emotion and that at the time of death many strong feelings are at work in life. It might well help people face the significance of the feelings that exist, without playing upon them in a way that would be dramatic or lacking in consideration.

The meditation should speak with courage and directness about the thoughts and feelings that exist in the presence of death, but it should not do this to stimulate guilt but rather to help persons understand and work through any guilt feelings they may have. It should speak of the great verities of the faith that are in sharp focus during times of emotional stress. And while it must have intellectual respectability, there should be no effort to belittle or deny the feelings that exist.

Through the years I have made it a practice to make each funeral service unique. No two were ever alike. While many of the same prayers and Scripture readings were so important that they had to be used repeatedly, the service was designed to recognize that a unique being had died, and those present were to be aware of the fact that in the eyes of the church and its pastor this uniqueness was clearly recognized. While often the funeral meditation made no reference to the person who had died, it always sought to speak directly to the needs of those who had come to share the service.

After many years of experience, it seems that the one thing that has stood out has been the many expressions of appreciation for the fact that the service had a personal quality, although it might not have any personal reference. Persons are often justifiably concerned lest comments should be made that are not accurate or are not acceptable to those who knew the deceased. This need never be the case when the meditation is directed toward the resources available for the bereaved.

In the series of meditations that follow, ten have no specific reference to the person who has died. They are designed to recognize the presence of death and the needs of those who face the fact. Ten others are built around some greater or lesser recognition of the life and interests of the person involved. In some it is touched on only lightly, and in others it becomes the organization point for all that is said.

The services that were more sharply focused still kept the primary concern on the privilege of presenting Christian truth as it relates to human need. With the suicide, the tragic accident, the child, the problem was more specific, so the treatment was also. With the school teacher, the sea captain, and the scientist, it was a personal reference that related the person who had died to the truth that was being interpreted. With the polio victim and the prominent man in the community, the well-known qualities of the person who had died were points for illustration without becoming what would be called personal references. The memorial service meditation indicates what may be done with those occasions where the nature of the group and the occasion call for a somewhat different treatment.

These meditations are not presented as models as much as they are indications of what one person with obvious limitations has tried to do to make the funeral service a significant personal and spiritual experience for those who shared in it. It goes without saying that each pastor will develop for himself the mode of expression and the nature of presentation that best conforms to his pastoral concern and his theological insight. This is as it should be. The following examples may serve as a guide or a form of critique for the pastor who works to develop his own use of tradition, liturgy, and personal practice.

JESUS WEPT

MEDITATION AT THE SERVICE FOR
A BELOVED SCHOOL TEACHER

Our feelings are close to the surface today. It would not
take much for them to come welling up and pouring out.
And let me say to you that these feelings we share today are
a good thing.

In our day we have built up the attitude that there is
something wrong or unhealthy about strong feelings. We
become embarrassed when we see others expressing their
feelings vigorously, and we try to place checks upon the
outpouring of our own emotions. We are taught that good
scouts do not cry, as if there were something heroic about
denying our feelings.

I am sure that we would all agree that there are some
emotions that are unwise and inappropriate and that these
had better be kept in check, but the feelings that bring us
together today are quite different. Grief is an honorable
emotion, for it grows from our love. We invest ourselves in
love and in consequence run the risk of loss and bereave-

45

ment. But the choice of avoiding this kind of loss would be the denial of love, and this would impoverish life unspeakably.

So we are talking about the powerful and positive feelings that relate to our own self-giving in love. These are the best parts of ourselves, and we cannot deny the best within us without doing damage to its development. How then can we cope with these feelings so that they are expressed with human dignity but also with respect for what they are?

In matters like these we do not go astray if we look to the Scriptures and the life of our Master for guidance. It is twice recorded that Jesus wept. One of these instances came when it was quite clear that Jerusalem, so centered in its own political and commercial life, was unresponsive to the message of Jesus. He looked over the city he loved and poured out tears of grief that it had denied its destiny. This was the expression of love and love's disappointment for a large group of people.

The other time was when Jesus visited Mary and Martha after the apparent death of their brother Lazarus. Jesus stood with the sisters and unashamedly wept. Interestingly, those who stood near were quick to interpret his behavior, for they said, "See how he loved him!" The expression of grief has been traditionally accepted as an expression of affection. What happens when the denial of grief produces the opposite form of behavior?

Perhaps we should make it clear that our feelings are an integral part of ourselves with their own validity. We do not decide whether or not we will have feelings. They exist. What we do often try to decide is whether or not these feelings will be expressed. The expression of our feelings is a form of organic behavior. We have the choice of expressing our feelings in wise and healthy ways, so that our love and concern can be communicated, or we can repress our feelings, only to find them coming around by some detour to find other and perhaps less acceptable forms of expression. In fact, physicians point out that many illnesses are the organic expression of feelings that have been denied expression normally, so that they were forced to find indirect and abnormal modes of expression.

One of the hazards of our day of sophisticated behavior is that we tend to become afraid of our own emotions. We try to blot them out by artificial means. It is not strange in our emotional climate that the use of tranquilizers, sedation, and popular forms of bottled anesthesia are at a high level of consumption. These are the ways by which we try to blot out our feelings. But it doesn't work. We tend either to destroy our capacity to feel right feelings, or we destroy ourselves in the process.

Our Master was always sensitive to those who had strong feelings, even when they might not be handled well. He was quite willing to express his own feelings with candor, openly and unashamed. He knew that feelings were an important part of being and had to be respected for what they were, a significant form of human behavior. Should we do less?

Perhaps more than we realize there is something significant taking place here this afternoon. We have come together, at one place and at one time, to recognize strong feelings that we have in common and to support each other in our expression of them. This is one of the important functions of the Christian community, and it is part of the self-verifying practice of specialized worship. There has never been a service like this before in human history nor will there ever be another one like it. This service is unique in the presence of the physical vessel within which our dear friend lived and from which she took leave but a few short days ago. This service is her service, because it is compounded of our feelings for her. This we would not deny, and of this we are not ashamed.

Perhaps the reason why so many of us are here today is that we felt the genuine warmth of emotion emanating from the life of a concerned person. Our lives were touched by it, and they glowed a little brighter because of it. The fine emotion of her nature enriched all life about her. It would have been tragic for us if she had successfully concealed or denied her feelings throughout her life. It would be similarly tragic if we so bound up our good feelings that no one knew we had them. Our world suffers for the kind of warmth she shed abroad. Perhaps if there is anything we can learn from her now, it is that we have a right to our good feelings and we have a right to express them without dismay, for they are an important part of our being. Let us pass on to others that quality of feeling we so much valued in her life as a living memorial for which we need not feel ashamed.

NO MORE DEATH, NEITHER SORROW

MEDITATION USED AT THE SERVICE FOR
AN ELDERLY SEA CAPTAIN

My friends, you share with me today a chance to recognize our obligation to and affection for a rare human being. As a sea captain, our friend interspersed his periods of time with us by long and interesting journeys to far parts of our world. He was not a stranger to distant places, and he was well acquainted with those places that are to us unknown. It may well be that there is a parable for us that can help us to penetrate in some measure the mystery of death.

Our friend, the captain, traveled always in close contact with two aspects of reality, which at first seem to be incompatible yet in reality are ever interdependent. He was well aware of those things we call "real"—the solid metal of the hull of his ship, the weighty engines that furnished the power to turn the propellers under the water. He knew so well the strength of the wind and the power of the waves. His course was set so that he would avoid the hazard of the rocks and shoals but would find the safety of the port, which was his goal.

Yet while he was well aware of the physical things about him, he was a competent skipper because he was always responsive to something else, the unseen and unseeable. He had early learned to use the sextant, so that he could tell where he was by his relationship to the stars. Also he knew how to use the compass, that sensitive instrument that maintains its right relationship with the magnetic pole and by so doing gives a clear sense of direction. With the improvements of navigational equipment and the development of electronics, he began to use yet more refined instruments that could reach into the apparent emptiness about him and pick up those signals, words, and pictures that fixed his position and verified his course. With his radar he could see through fog and darkness to the sharply defined rocks, shores, and other vessels. All of this represented a refined skill, in living with a world of energy, to use that energy wisely.

When we recognize the ability of man to function in two quite different but complementary levels of existence, we can see something about the meaning of death that often escapes us. To a sea captain working within both spheres —material things and energy forms—it would have seemed a futile and useless thing to argue as to which was the more important. A ship needed to be seaworthy, but it also needed to be sensitive to the unseen. Both were essential to its safe arrival in port.

Actually we are quite ignorant about death. We see the end of physical life, and from that we postulate all kinds of meanings. But we are also sure that life is made up of a combination of things both physical and spiritual. It may well be that the spiritual keeps on functioning even after the material is brought safely into port. For the ultimate reality is not to be found in the things that can break down or be destroyed but rather in the things that cannot suffer destruction.

Our concern would be then with the development of those things that have the mark of the eternal upon them even in the midst of time. Here again, the sea captain has built up a dependence upon things beyond himself that can be symbolic for us. The navigator of the sea regularly uses three aids that work together to guide him—his charts, his compass, and the system of lights along the shore. The analogy for those aids that guide the life of the seeking Christian is quite obvious.

The Christian's chart is the Bible, an accumulation of the experience of men who have gone before to chart the blessings and the hazards of human life. With care and honesty these sacred pages spell out for us the high lands and the low, the safe passages and the rocky shores. No one can navigate without reference to the experience of those who have gone before and mapped their course for us.

But the map in itself is never enough, for we need to know where we are in relation to the map. The mariner uses the compass to help establish his position in relation to the shore. The seeking Christian uses the sensitivity created by prayer to help him honestly face himself and so ascertain his position in relation to life and its important events.

But the map and the compass are dependent upon a final fix that comes when the navigator seeks the safe entrance into port. Here he relates himself to the lights along the shore. These lights, by their size, shape, and color, fix upon the chart and guide him through the channel. Jesus has been called the beacon light of history, and the Scriptures speak of him as "the light of the world." The insights of human history and the sensitivities that are gained through prayer are made specific as we measure our lives by the example and teaching of this source of divine revelation, Jesus, whose experience of God was so real. It is difficult for us to get lost in the fog of doubt or the darkness of fear when we keep our eyes focused on that light that lighteth every man that comes into the world.

Our friend, the captain, was a man of rugged faith. He had learned through rigorous experience the need for a healthy balance between independence, self-assurance, and courage, and the qualities of dependence, self-surrender, and openness for guidance. His life continues to speak of what he believed. In our tribute to him may we also be responsive to what he would most surely say to us were he yet able: if we would keep from the rocks and safely make the port, we should develop our sensitivity to the things of the spirit. We should draw from the insight of the past, refine it through our own sensitivity in the present, and measure it by the finest standard we know, the person of Jesus, the Christ.

ARROWS ARE SHARP IN THE HEART

MEDITATION USED AT THE SERVICE
CONDUCTED AFTER SUICIDE

Today we are met under a double burden. We not only face the specter of untimely and tragic death, but we carry that extra burden of guilt that comes when we say to ourselves, when there is no one about to hear, "What could I have done that this untoward event might not have happened?"

You and I know that pretty words now would bring little comfort, for the pain in our beings is beyond the reach of the superficial. Rather it is for us to face the full impact of this hour and then be in the proper mood to receive the full measure of strength and guidance that our religion affords us.

The phrase that the Psalmist used in quite a different context seems appropriate for us today, for we feel set upon by a stern judgment, and our hearts are pierced by the arrows of our sorrow. While we would in no way minimize our anguished feelings, it is more important for us to ask, "What can we say to them?"

53

At the very least, we recognize that it is the mark of our finite nature that we do not see or understand or interpret wisely all of the communications that come to us from the troubled life of another. We become so immersed in the tasks of the day that our perception becomes dulled, and we do not see clearly the signs that are given or hear well the cries of another. And although we would not excuse ourselves too easily from the obligations of our humanity, we know that we are not all-wise or all-knowing. The marks and limitations of our finiteness are clearly upon us.

We also recognize that the burden of guilt hangs heavily upon us, for we know that we are interrelated and inter-dependent, and when something ill happens to one, it in a measure happens to all. But we also know that our feelings here are the sign both of our burden and of our salvation, for it takes a highly developed moral sensitivity to be aware of the burden and to carry it with courage. Just as grief is the other side of the coin of love, so feelings of guilt are the other side of the coin of moral responsibility.

There is the guilt that we can relieve by the acts of resti-tution. We can do good to another for the injury we have done. We can pay the debt with interest. We can ask and receive forgiveness. This is the normal way for us to meet the burdens of real guilt. This is the way of the Lord's Prayer with its recognition of the reciprocal relationship between failure and forgiveness: Forgive as we forgive. But when death intervenes, and we cannot do the acts of restitution directly, what then? We use our feelings to build up that reservoir of right relationships and good will from which mankind draws its needed supply of under-standing and kindliness. The good that we would have done another, and cannot, can become the good that we would do in his name even though he cannot. In this way even our being becomes a living memorial.

But being human as we are, we tend to be our own worst critics. We condemn ourselves in a way that we would resent were another to do it to us. We say sharp things to ourselves and even punish ourselves, often for things we did not do. We need to take a long, cool look at feelings like these, for they do no one good. They fill us with fear and apprehension that can deteriorate into depression, and they serve no useful purpose. No one is helped when we chastise ourselves for things we only imagine we did. No restitution accrues from the acts of self-punishment that are products of our tortured imagination. For often in our moments of emotional crisis, we reach back into the past for some thought or act with which to assail ourselves, and it has no bearing on fact or reality. It serves no purpose in righting the wrongs of life. We must be on guard against the emotional pitfall that could lead us to plead guilty of offenses we have not done, for we must remember that such pleading does no one good. This is the time when we need to stand together in mutual understanding and good will.

Yet even more than these things is the simple fact of our humanity and its limitations. We all know that we are finite beings, marked by the limitations of our mortal natures. When another dies, we are reminded of the fact that our lives are marked in space and time, and we become restless. We feel within us the ideal of perfection, and we know we so often fall short of it. We feel that something in us is attuned to eternal things, yet the burden of the days with their trivial rounds of activities often blots out the higher vision. And we feel guilt because we know we are not all that we should be. But this, too, can be carried too far, for we cannot deny our nature, and claim for ourselves in this life the achievements that come with a life of eternal and infinite dimensions. Here we know that we stand in need of the grace of God that keeps giving us another tomorrow as a time when we can practice the good we know. For surely we would learn of our shortcomings in the past, but we would not let these weigh so heavily upon us that we would move into the future crippled by our burden.

When we are burdened with the feelings expressed in that oft-repeated phrase, "If only I had known," we need to lay hold of certain truths made clear for us in the New Testament. Some of the illnesses of life reach more deeply into the core of our beings than we are aware. These are not times for blame but rather the instances through which the power of God can be revealed at work in the lives of those who trust in him. Our Master was quick to forgive, especially when he saw that persons wanted to know and do the right. To forgive is to give back the future, what lies before. Persons came to him in all states of mind and emotion, and he made it his task to help them receive the healing, redeeming love of God, that washed away the painful past and opened the doors toward a future that was more nearly God's will.

We stand today as one in our sadness over the events of the past. But we have it in our power through the teachings of our faith to accept the pain, reorganize our living, and move into the future free of unreasonable burdens and more fully aware of the grace of God that speaks directly to every human need.

ON FINISHING THE COURSE

St. Paul says in Second Timothy, "The time of my departure has come. I have fought the good fight, I have finished the race, I have kept the faith." For him these seem to have been the points of measurement for his life. Perhaps more than we realize they become the yardstick for all of us. Today it seems particularly appropriate that we center our thought on the valid testimony of the Christian faith in the presence of death on these words of St. Paul.

The one to whom we pay our debt of respect and affection today was no stranger to adversity. From early in life she bore the burden of a crippling physical handicap. Every step was a painful experience for her and a distressing sight for us to behold. She might well have used this handicap, so visible and so distressing, as a legitimate excuse to beat a retreat from life. Few would have blamed her had she chosen so to do. But it was not in her nature to do that. She was well aware of the struggle implicit in her living.

57

It must have been a continual fight to bring her crippled body under the control of her unflagging spirit, but she kept at it, and instead of retreating early to a wheelchair, she advanced into life on many fronts, fighting a good fight against adversity.

With such a burden to bear, it must have been a continual battle within to keep from surrender. No one would have blamed her if at any time during the course of recent years she had decided she had done enough, that no more was expected of her, and she could have made an easy retirement into the seclusion of her home where she could have been cared for. But that was not her nature. Not two weeks ago she called me and said, "If you are driving down past the nursing home today, I would very much appreciate a ride. This is my day to read." While she had resources to use, she used them—and not for herself alone but for others. How our friends at the nursing home will miss her on those days when she came in to read to them by the hour! She made them feel that somebody cared and was willing to suffer a little more that they might suffer a little less. She kept this attitude until she had used up her strength. She ran the race to the finish.

And she kept the faith. We hear this phrase quite often, but I wonder if we understand it. A faith is not something we keep like a memento, a source of interest and occasional reference. A faith is something we keep as we would keep a garden. It is a living and growing thing, but it must be continually cultivated. I am sure that she would be happy to bequeath her faith to us.

What was her faith like? How did it work? What did she do to keep it vital and alive?

To begin with, she had faith in herself. That is not as

easy as it sounds. It is easy to be filled with self-doubt. She could have had plenty of that if she had wanted to use her handicap. But she kept her faith in herself by a discipline that expected more of herself than anyone else expected of her. One day she told me about it. She said the first thing she did in the morning was to plan something unusual and interesting for the day and then make sure she did it. It might be a book to read, a letter to write, or a visit to make. But no day was an empty routine for her. Each day was lived with a goal. In this way she kept her faith in herself alive. She kept her life from becoming ordinary. She made living important.

Then, too, she cultivated her faith in other people. In her condition it was easy to feel offended or excluded. She had to learn that people are often embarrassed by circumstances they cannot cope with, and so an extra effort has to be made to understand them. She had a simple rule for keeping her faith in other people. It was this: No matter what a person did, she tried to apply to it the best possible motive. She said this made it easier to understand people, but I am sure it also made it easier for her to keep her faith in others. Often we downgrade others by excessive and unreasonable criticisms. We do not seem to realize that, at the same time, we are downgrading our capacity to have faith in others.

But most of all, she kept her faith in God. It was a simple faith. She would not have been at home in a classroom where the intricacies of theology were being discussed. For her it was enough to believe that under and above and all around her there was something eternally good that she could trust. Even if life had seemed to deal her a cruel blow, she attributed it to the shortcomings of man and his knowledge of disease, and not to any evil purpose working itself out in human affairs. She was the most enthusiastic person I knew when it came to appreciating the new vaccine for polio. She could understand what it would mean to many to be spared what had happened to her. But hers was never a mood of bitterness or resentment. Rather it was one of increased joy when she found that man's wisdom and knowledge had discovered what she was sure God wanted revealed all the time. Yes, her faith was not complicated, but it was durable, and it never let her down.

We are here today because we share a common respect and affection for a noble spirit that lived in a sadly crippled little body. Yet that spirit was always in control. It is not difficult for us to believe now that she has laid aside the burden of this flesh and is faring forth in that disciplined and adventurous faith that stood her so well while she was among us. Yet we feel sure that she would continue to speak to us of her faith, not through exhortation for that had no part in her, but through her being, which reached out in responsiveness to all around her.

Yes, she fought a good fight, she finished her course, and she kept her faith well.

WHERE ARE THE HORIZONS?

MEDITATION USED AT THE SERVICE
FOR A RESEARCH SCIENTIST

When we stand in the presence of death, we are obliged to readjust our thinking to new horizons. We are so used to living in terms of material things and to using the clearly discernible landmarks about us to fix our place in space and time that we are forced into quite a different way of looking at things when we examine the spaceless and the timeless. Death forces us to do that, for the human being we have known no longer has a body that fills space and a life span that is measured by clocks and calendars.

We have just prayed a prayer that said, "Death is only a horizon, and a horizon is nothing save the limit of our sight. So clear our eyes that we may see those things that death cannot take from us." Just what did those words mean?

Man is continually struggling to come to terms with his horizons. Airplane pilots have a special instrument that can show them their horizons when they are surrounded by clouds. They can only navigate correctly when they have a point of reference that is dependable. So it is with us. We have to be sure of our horizons before we can be sure of anything else.

But this is not as easily done as said. The whole history of man's progress has been the outgrowing of small frames of reference, so that he could accommodate his mind and spirit to new and wider horizons.

In medieval times men were comfortable in a cozy universe centered about the earth. Then came Copernicus with his theory of a universe centered about the sun, and Galileo proved it with his telescope. Then men had to go through the painful process of adjusting their thinking to a larger and more impersonal universe. But it was done, and man's concept of the nature of God grew with the necessity of expanded vision.

In the nineteenth century, with the development of the biological sciences, man began to question his unique creation. Evidence piled up that he was not separated from the rest of living things, but that he was rather very much a part of the natural order, sharing its characteristics with all living things. This tended to deny the theory of a special creation for man, and at first this was quite a shattering blow to his dignity. But with time he realized that his creation was a far more significant and complicated process, and he gained not only a new sense of his uniqueness but also an understanding of his relationship to all creation.

Man's next important horizon was his own mind. He had always had the feeling that his mind was an unquestioned and dependable source of insight and truth. Then came the studies of the scientists of personality, which pointed out that the mind of man was a far more complicated and less understandable instrument than he had assumed. But, instead of letting this destroy his faith in himself, man found new bases for understanding those elements of his being that in the past had been baffling. He began to know how wonderfully and fearfully he was made.

Then came the discoveries of the physical scientists—that the universe as we knew it was not built of crude matter but was rather a magnificent construct of infinite energy in fantastic patterns and designs that could be traced through all creation, in the stars as well as in ourselves. The sense of cosmic unity was given scientific credence, and man with his comprehending mind seemed to be situated at the summit of consciousness.

All of these new horizons faced by man called for new and vigorous ways of thinking about himself and his universe, and all of them come together here and now to help us as we adjust ourselves to the horizon that death forces upon us. The thing that always seemed so frightening about death was its finality and its impenetrability. Now some of the horizons seem to be more clearly and understandably fixed.

All that we can understand of the explorations of science points out for us that the universe is more like a great thought than a great thing. Therefore, the thinking creature is more at home in it. The universe is essentially organized energy, and so is the spiritual nature of man. This seems to mean that man as a spiritual being, unique in his God-consciousness, is more at home in the universe than he had imagined, for his essential nature and the nature of the universe are one.

This means, then, that as we stand in the presence of death, we are dealing with the physical illusion, when in truth we should be coping with the ultimate spiritual truth. The horizons we face are not those of physical change as much as they are the release of spiritual energy. For the new point of focus that leads toward the understanding of human experience is the nature of man as a creature capable of God-consciousness and a cosmic being, able to be revealed through wisdom, order, and purpose and the capacity for meaningful relationship between the two.

If the point of ultimate meaning for life is found at the point of relationship between the God-perceiving man and the self-revealing God, we then grasp the simple fact that death as an incident in the biological history of a man is hardly relevant to this basic relationship. In fact, it may well be that the process of dying and the event of physical death may release the spiritual energy of the individual so that the ultimate of the creature–creator relationship can be achieved.

The mind of man has from earliest times been baffled by the meaning of death. Yet he has always had the feeling that physical death was in some way separated from the core of his being, so that while he might taste of death, he was never devoured by it. The far vistas revealed to us by the latest discoveries of man tend to verify this "invincible surmise" of the soul. For while we stand in the presence of death, we do not feel conquered by it. When we stand at our full spiritual stature, we do not measure our living by a biological event. Rather we measure it by the truth that is revealed in and through us. This truth is that there is something in man that was not made to die but rather finds its meaning beyond the measurements of time and space. For from its beginning it had upon it the marks of the infinite and eternal.

LET US NOW PRAISE GREAT MEN

MEDITATION USED AT THE SERVICE FOR A
PROMINENT MAN IN THE COMMUNITY

When we take the time to think about it, we all know that death can be different. For death is not merely an event in the function of a highly complicated biological entity. It is also the final chapter in the private history of an individual. Therefore it has its own meaning. It may well draw that meaning from the context of the life that has been lived.

We are met here today to pay our tribute of respect and affection to one who has walked among us with dignity and integrity for many years. I was careful not to say our final tribute, for his life has been so intertwined with creative activities in this community that both directly and indirectly we will long continue to support and pay tribute to those things that he initiated. Without being aware of the fact, he built his memorials in the hearts and minds of men, women, and children.

His concern for the youth of the community has been

expressed by his determined effort, while a member of the Board of Education, to provide a fine new school. When he served as chairman of the Park Commission, he reclaimed lands and put to new use those places that could well have become a blight to our neighborhood but now with new beauty have turned the desert to a place of springs that it may blossom as the rose. These things we recognize and appreciate.

But our purpose here today is not to pay tribute to his public life as much as to recognize his faith and its meaning for his life. His four score years, minus two, were lived in this place. Blessed by the fortune of good ancestors, he gave to his inheritance the benefits of his own mind and spirit, so that, as if he had made a gentleman's agreement with life, he worked diligently to give back more than he had received. But it was not so much what he did as how he did it that will linger in our memories. With that fortunate combination of true maturity and clear purpose, he moved quietly but assuredly toward the goals he had set. Yet always there was an understanding of others and an appreciation of their differences that represented a capacity for true acceptance of others.

This quality of his life is the logical expression of his basic philosophy of life, for he had early discerned the heart of the Christian concept of the sacredness of all life and the obligation to value the lives of others, even when it might be most difficult. It has often been observed that he held as dear friends those who differed with him most sharply in matters of policy. And we have often commented upon the fact that, in these recent years, he and his most vigorous competitor have spent their vacation month in the South together. These things bespeak a breadth and depth of human understanding that could hardly exist apart from a basic meaning for life that grew from his interpretation of the Christian faith.

We have good reason to believe that even the quality of death itself was for him different because of his way of life. For him death came not as an enemy stalking him through his years of failing strength, but rather it came as a friend in whom he could trust for further revealed meaning, quite as he had trusted life. For he approached death as he had approached life, with openness and expectancy, believing that it was God's will to make available to his children that which could fulfill the finest possibilities of being.

This quality of mind and spirit was expressed in a visit I had with him just a few days before his death. He spoke quite candidly. He said, "I think my old body is running down. This time I don't think the doctors are going to find a way to give it another boost of energy. But that's all right. We've gotten along together for a long time, and I can tell it needs a rest. But, you know, the closer I get to the end, the less apprehension I feel about it. There was a time when I wanted very much to live, but now I feel my work is over, and I am quite ready to go."

These are the words of a person whose life and death have a unity. He approached death as he had approached life—with a desire to make it creative and useful. For him it was not a time when a break occurred between what he was and what he would be. They were one and indivisible. Integrity of being and underlying faith ran through both life and death to make them one.

It would be presumptive of us to pass any judgment upon life or to feel that any words we could utter could add one cubit to its measure. But it does seem an expression of our own need as we stand in the presence of death, to see that it can be a final chapter in a personal history that is written with coherence and complete integrity. For truly he died as he had lived. It was an experience into which he projected the same kind of meaning that he had found in life. He lived a man of faith, and when his allotted time ran out, he also died a man of faith.

What does a life like his have to say to us? We know that when anyone dies some part of us also faces death. We know that in its spiritual dimension life is indivisible. We also know that when a good man dies, he says something to us in death as he has spoken to us in life. Perhaps he would say that life as we know it is surrounded by the impenetrable mysteries of birth and death, and that even while we live, we walk the narrow edge of mystery. But behind the mystery and among the impenetrable shadows, his faith said that he was not alone, for God stood "within the shadows keeping watch above his own."

So we come not as those overborne by tragedy, but rather as those who would pronounce a benediction upon a life well lived and well died. And we would feel that our own existence takes on heightened meaning as we perceive the quality of that faith that adds value to all of the experience of life, even that closing event, so wrapped in mystery, which we call death.

MY GOD, WHY?

MEDITATION USED AT THE SERVICE FOLLOWING
THE TRAGIC DEATH OF FINE YOUNG MAN

We are gathered here today under what I am quite sure we would all agree are most tragic circumstances. When a young life—rich in promise, in the midst of significant and uncompleted tasks—is brought to death, we are stunned by the overpowering emotions of the event. When that young life is closely bound up with ours in the intimate relationships and rewarding friendships of life, we feel threatened by the event that has taken away his life.

It is not strange, then, that there should well up from deep within our beings that agonizing question, "My God, why?" For at first glance these tragic and untimely events seem to violate the wisdom and justice that we like to believe is basic to the cosmic order. When something so basic is challenged, we feel threatened and insecure. Because we are geared to the just, we feel threatened by injustice. Because we are rooted in reason, we feel uncertain in the presence of the unreasonable. Because our faith is in the

69

goodness of God, we feel the special hazard of those things that are so clearly evil.

What then can we say to these things? How can we and our faith stand secure in the evil hour? Because these questions are uppermost in our minds and because they need answers, I will try to speak to them now.

Our faith expresses itself through the belief that it is God's plan for man to find fulfillment, an abundant life. We are assured in the Scriptures that it is not God's will that one of his children should suffer. Yet we are also aware of the fact that man in the exercise of his freedom is continually doing those things that compromise God's will and bring consequences to life that are filled with injustice, suffering, and evil.

Our friend was exercising his freedom of choice in being where he was at the time of tragedy. He was there on a mission of mercy because he was that kind of man. We would certainly not want to limit or curtail the ability to express freedom in that way. But the course of events implies that another person was also employing the same privilege of freedom destructively, so that he was at the same place, befogged in mind and judgment, uncontrolled in thought and action. He employed his freedom to use an easily accessible anesthetic for purposes that seemed sufficiently good to him, even though this showed his disregard for the rights and safety of others. Man's freedom can be used to destroy as well as to fulfill.

The quality of being that separates our human nature from the rest of nature is the privilege and responsibility of our freedom. We glory in the privileges of this freedom for it is the mark of a man. We are ofttimes restive under the responsibility of our freedom, for it too often becomes the measure of man. And faced with this measurement, we are aware of our shortcomings.

This tragic moment is not separated from the mainstream of human tragedy, for in it we see in sharp focus that evidence of human shortcoming which in some degree marks all of us. Yet in honesty of spirit we cannot blame this on God, for to do so would be to deny the source of our faith and the basis for our impulse to fulfill the responsibilities of our nature.

It is at times like these that our Christian faith urges upon us the demands for forgiveness and the obligations to seek "grace for this and every time of need," for which we earnestly pray. Yet our prayer is invariably an expression of our doubt as well as of our faith. Our faith is never an easy achievement, but rather the struggle of our best insight against the fears and failures that mark our mortal natures.

Perhaps we see this most clearly in that prayer of our Lord, uttered in his suffering upon the cross. His witness to his faith had led through rejection and betrayal to execution at the hands of brutal men in a careless system. His witness must at times have seemed to be a desperately lonely expression of faith in a world that was unprepared to understand it. How human were those words which echoed the cry of the Psalmist, "My God, my God, why hast thou forsaken me?"

Yet as we look closely at the words, we realize that they were more than a cry of despair. They were also a cry of faith directed in the mood and spirit of prayer. They affirmed a confidence in a God who was responsive to our agony of spirit as well as to our highest aspirations. For our faith is not made to deal only with life at its best. It also is geared to the needs of life at its worst.

Because our Master was able to cry out in his loneliness and despair to a God who was near enough to pray to, even when it was an anguished prayer, he was able to go on in that high level of human understanding which could say, "Father, forgive them; for they know not what they do," and ultimately make that affirmation of faith that said, "Father, into thy hands I commend my spirit."

This, then, is not the time for us to be so overwhelmed by the tragedy of life that we lose sight of the spiritual resources that are needed most when life is at its darkest hour. But, rather, this is the time when we share the common responsibility for our human shortcomings and the perpetual need for that divine grace, which can help us to fulfill more wisely the obligations of our humanity as we also share the privileges of faith and freedom.

No one would try to deny the heavy burden of this hour, but we would be careful not to deny also the strength that is accessible for meeting it. If we turn against God when our need is greatest, we compound the tragedy. For although our cry, "My God, why?" is the natural expression of our suffering, it can also be part of the answer to our need. Our freedom for failure is a part of our nature, but so also is our privilege of calling upon that healing, redeeming love of God, which does not limit us by those marks of our humanity, but places within us the capacity to grow through tragedy to a fuller understanding of the obligations of our humanity and the resources of our faith.

In our faith, and in the strength of that faith, let us stand firm in the hour of suffering in the knowledge that, although the good suffer and the innocent often bear heavy burdens, it is the mark of man's failure and not the will of God that is made manifest. For the anguished cry of the 22nd Psalm is followed by the trust and assurance of the 23rd: "The Lord is my shepherd, I shall not want."

EXCEPT YE BECOME AS A CHILD

MEDITATION USED AT THE SERVICE FOLLOWING THE DEATH OF A CHILD

Matt. 18:1-6

Intro: It is a basic element of our faith that we can find meaning even in what appears to be most meaningless. Victor Frankl, writing of his experience in a German concentration camp, tells how he urged those who shared the wretched experience with him to struggle always to give full human dignity even to the tragic circumstances of life, for only then would they be able to go on with the tasks of living. When those who were brought near to death and utter hopelessness asked him what meaning there might be in their plight, he urged them to seek some beauty, some remembrance, some hope to cling to, for in it they would be able to affirm their human superiority over the destructiveness that was so evident all about them.

We meet today with a need to reaffirm our faith, for we need it so desperately. Perhaps nothing tests our faith so relentlessly as the death of a child, with the young life so ruthlessly plucked from among us while it was yet so clearly

74

untried and unfulfilled. We want so much for our children that we seem doubly tried when death disrupts our hopes and our plans.

What then can we say to these things? Where can we find some beauty, some remembrance, some hope to cling to?

One day Jesus was talking with his disciples about the nature of God's kingdom. He called a youngster to him and said that unless his hearers were able to take on the attributes of a child, they would not be able to know the meaning of God's kingdom. What could he have meant?

 One of the things we notice first about a child is his openness and responsiveness. He is not only willing to receive but is completely unashamed and unabashed in his asking. How often when we return from shopping will we be met at the door by a child with the question, "What did you get for me?" His desire to receive is open and unqualified.

Too often, as we grow older, we build up defenses against receiving, because we feel that to accept carries an obligation to give back. One of the marks of maturity is the ability to accept responsibility and fulfill obligations. But we err if we believe this quality of human obligation must be applied in the same way to our relationship to God. For the gifts of God are so unbounded that we deny much of life's opportunity if we feel that we will only receive of God insofar as we are able to pay back. This attitude can separate us from God at the point where our need is greatest. We can never pay our debts to God. We can only in small measure be aware of them. But we can, as far as possible, stand in the presence of God with openness of mind and spirit, that in his wisdom and providence our needs may

be met. Let us not now allow small judgments and petty
fears to stand between us in our need for God's presence in
the depth of our being.

II. Another thing about a child that we see so clearly is
his utter and unrestrained dependence. He is helpless without the emotional and physical support of the adults around
him. He is not ashamed of his helplessness but accepts it
without question. When he grows older, he assumes more
and more independence, and sometimes we regret this
growth. Sometimes this increased dependence on physical
things also asserts itself in spiritual matters. We seek to be
independent of our need for God. Jesus evidently warned
against this unwise use of independence, for it tends to
separate man from his source of spiritual strength. We do
not ultimately find our security in a way of thinking and
feeling that blinds us to our mortal nature and makes us
unaware of our dependence upon a cosmic Other for the
meaning of life itself.

III. Yet another characteristic of a child is his unbounded
sense of wonder. Life and its experiences are new. Everything about him is unknown and to be explored. This
capacity for wonder is the basic ingredient of worship, the
giving of worth to life. One of the hazards of maturity is
that we lose this sense of wonder and with it the capacity
to find new meaning for life. Let us not close our minds
and spirits to this capacity to seek meaning and wonder
even in the things that distress us, for these too may be
vehicles for a growing meaning if we allow them to be.

It has long been observed that similar events may produce differing meanings for persons, depending upon how
they are willing to accept the events. To fight against life
is to open the doors to bitterness, resentment, and ill will.

To accept even those things that are painful and tragic with a determination to grow through them brings to life understanding, mellowness, and a deepening of faith. One of the more difficult choices of life is the one we make when we decide how we will let life's events mold us.

What does our faith say to us in a moment of tragic disappointment such as this? Today we have set before us the life of a little child—by our measurements incomplete and denied the possibilities of fulfillment. But we also have set before us an opportunity to see more clearly than ever before the measurements of a spiritual kingdom, not gauged by the man-made yardsticks of space and time; an opportunity to see those qualities of openness and acceptance of life, the nature of a complete and unrestrained dependence, and through it all, some of the unquenchable wonder that gives to life its glory and its beauty.

"Unless you become like children." Here the emphasis is on becoming, the open door to meaning. While we lament those circumstances so incident to our mortal natures, we cannot close our eyes to those spiritual meanings that can be revealed to us and through us as we choose to make our lives an experience of unending spiritual growth. For it may well be that in that growth we prepare ourselves for the processes of restoration which build up for us a spiritual treasure that nothing known to earth can destroy.

This is our faith. This we need to believe most vigorously when it is most difficult. So our faith speaks to us, even now.

RESURRECTION AND LIFE

MEDITATION AT THE SERVICE FOR A CHURCH
SCHOOL TEACHER

We meet this afternoon in this hallowed place where
we have so often come together in the past. But today
our coming together is different. We have never been here
before for this purpose, and we will never be here again
for this same purpose. For we are met now to show our
respect and affection for a unique person, who walked
among us with dignity and honor, and who although now
claimed by death will continue to exist in our minds and in
our spirits. We knew him as both an engineer and a teacher
in our church school for many years. His legacy in instruc-
tion of the youth of the parish is a rich one.

Our friend was a man of inquiring intellect. He never
taught anything just because it was in the book. He had to
believe it himself before he would pass it on to another.
Thereby lies a story that may be instructive for us today,
for it speaks to our need as we look death squarely in the
face.

One day our friend called and said he wanted to talk with me about something that had been troubling him. It proved to be the idea of the Resurrection. He said that he knew it was in the ancient creed that he had learned as a boy, he knew it was in the Bible, but still the idea did not make sense to him. He said that he had skirted around it in his teaching, but space exploration and the direct questioning of his class members had made him face up to the subject as he had not done before. His question was simply this, "How can anyone nowadays believe in the resurrection of the body?"

We talked about the matter from many angles and came up with some answers that he accepted as satisfactory. Let us share them now.

At the outset we are faced by two simple facts. One is that the thought of the Resurrection was clearly the source of inspiration and vitality for the first-century church. It was the center of preaching, of witness, and of belief. But the simple fact is that it is the most difficult part of the Christian belief for us in the twentieth century to accept. It doesn't fit our world view, our idea of space, biology, or scientific belief. How then do we resolve the problem so that we can keep the inspiration without losing our intellectual integrity?

Perhaps it would help us to look again closely at the gospel record, for it presents a strange series of events. It tells of a visit to a cemetery and a missing body. Then it tells of a series of apparitions, supposedly of Jesus, but even members of his family and close friends did not recognize the vision. Then it tells of meetings with his disciples, during which he asked them to verify his wounds but came and went without opening the door. Also, on the road to Emmaus he walked with his disciples, and they did not recognize him until they ate supper together. Yet the impact of these strange events was to set the small group of disciples on fire so that they set about to transform the world.

It is very clear to us from the recounting of the events that they were not ordinary appearances, and the body was clearly a different body from the one he had known and his family and friends had known. Yet the quality of his spiritual body was so definite that the delayed recognition became doubly significant once their doubts were overcome.

If we are to approach this thing with psychological soundness, we must recognize that the law of cause and effect was at work in their behavior. Unless there had been a powerful cause, there could not have been such a history-making effect. It must have been in the meaning of the event for them. They had been filled with doubt; they had not believed the Master's words. They had run away in defeat and repeatedly denied even the fact that they knew him. Something happened to change all that. Now they were willing to suffer death for an idea and stake their reputations on an event that they witnessed.

The ancient world was filled with cults that sought to prove immortality, life after death. Interest in the subject was intense and widespread. So it was not strange that the idea of Christ's reappearance to his disciples would have been a matter of tremendous importance to them. It overcame their doubts about him and what he had said. It furnished them with the motive power to stand and affirm, where before they had denied and run away.

At the least we must admit that something important happened. St. Paul made a distinction between a physical and a spiritual body. He implied that the physical body has to be laid down in order to rise up with the spiritual body. He made other qualifications which show that he was speaking of a spiritual manifestation. He preached fervently the importance of the Resurrection, but for him it seemed to be this evidence of restored spiritual existence. He was close to the whole series of events that shook the first-century church. In fact, he was an important part of them. His firm belief in the power of the Resurrection upon the lives of men never seemed to get lost in mere body consciousness. For him it was clearly a spiritual event.

It is perhaps at this point that we can resolve the problem that confronts us. We cannot deny our modern views of science and the nature of the universe. We cannot do the impossible thing of accepting religious ideas that are essentially unacceptable, just to satisfy our emotional needs. But we can do something better. We can find in the important events of the disciples and the early church those meanings that are valid for us today. And they are these: The disciples discovered that there was something about their Master that was not destroyed by death. They felt this fact was a clue to the nature of man and his relationship to God. They believed so completely in the validity of this spiritual life that they lived with a reckless abandon as far as their own physical safety was concerned, for they felt sure that they would inherit this spiritual life. This belief has been close to the core of our faith for centuries. It does not deny anything we know about life. In fact it affirms the best we know of it. At a time like this, it seems particularly important to know that we are dealing with beginnings and not ends. A wise ancient teacher and a wise modern one see eye to eye on this point. So can we.

A MEMORIAL DAY

Far back in the Old Testament the value of a day of memory was proclaimed in regard to the Passover. "This day shall be for you a memorial day, and you shall keep it as a feast to the Lord." You are a part of an ancient and noble tradition, as you meet together this evening to pay a loving tribute to those who have walked among you and are no longer among the living, but a part of that far larger company, the dead.

Any memorial service is first of all a time of tribute. Within the bounds of this room you have learned the quality of character and experienced the sustaining nature of close friendship. What has been experienced in the lives of those with whom you have shared the privileges of friendship is not something temporary and fleeting. It is built into the depths of life. It has nourished your souls and it has done the same for those from among your group who have now taken up membership in another and wider fellowship. Although they are not here to share in the physical relationships of this hour, you cannot ever meet without their

82

presence. They have become a part of your existence. Whenever you share in that golden hour of recollection as the hands of the clock mark the hours that end the day, you are again part of an unbroken friendship. You feel again the presence of those who once were with you but have since gone on a while.

Memory is one of the qualities that makes life tolerable. Through this amazing power of the mind, you can reach into the past and reclaim for yourself its moments of high privilege and rich experience. It is our capacity for memory that makes possible the cumulative effect of our culture, and that passes on from generation to generation a new and greater amount of knowledge. The capacity to remember the quality of life of those who have gone before enriches the life of the present and inspires us for the future that lies yet before us. Life is full of the elements of tragedy and injustice, but there is a power of the human spirit that can rise above such experiences, to make them but incidents in a larger pattern of life. Memory makes it possible for that power of mind to exert itself. The mind rebuilds its treasured moments. It glories in them. The good that men do lives after them. It can be enhanced in the hearts and minds of those who treasure sacred memories.

But the mind is able not only to remember. Although it is not common among us, there is the capacity to foretell. Some look into the future and determine intelligent courses of action on the basis of reasoned prediction. Others seem to have a measure of intuition that defies rational explanation. Still others have so exact an insight into future events that they seem to destroy time, and live as it were on the threshold of eternity. When one has shared such a moment, he is never able again to live as he has before.

One morning at a Mediterranean base a young officer who was attached to the Air Force came to me in an anxious mood and said, "Tell me all you know about immortality and tell me quick." When I found out the nature of his concern, I explored with him an experience he had just had of seeing into the future with a clarity that defied reason. He was trained in the practical sciences; he had studied the workings of men's minds. Yet he said this unusual experience of preknowledge was the most real thing that had ever happened to him. He was to take off that afternoon with a planeload of litter cases for a base hospital. He said that he would experience difficulty with the plane, and at a spot he clearly foresaw the plane would plunge into a mountain, bringing death to those aboard. He went on to say that when it was over, he saw himself pull himself up out of the wreckage and set off by himself into the unknown.

We talked about his experience and the evidence that had accumulated that some persons had an ability to live beyond the measurements of time. We explored his religious insights and then I went with him to the airstrip as his plane prepared to take off. It was not an easy thing for him to go or for me to see him go. I was anxious about that flight all afternoon, and when the word was finally received by Operations concerning the end of that flight, it was just exactly as the young captain had recounted it to me that morning. I did not begin to understand all that was involved in such foreknowledge, but I had the feeling that I had been standing on sacred ground. For here was a man who in a real sense had experienced some of the timelessness that is a part of eternity.

Not many of us can see that clearly into future events, but each of us knows that the time must come when we shall take our place in the silent halls of death. It does not take unusual experience to give us a concern that we may be worthy of the responsibilities of brotherhood, whatever they may be for us.

But life is not only memory and foreknowledge. There is the reasoned living in the present that is made stronger by what we know has happened in the past and what will happen in the future. It is the power of ordered thought. It is a sense of cosmic design rather than chaotic lack of design. It is ordered living rather than disordered existence. It leads to a sense of purpose worthy of the privilege of living. It gives inspiration to work toward that purpose through the years of life allotted to us. It is the reasoned and balanced judgment that is basic to our faith in God and finds expression in our faith in man.

These three, memory, foreknowledge, and reason, become the bases for our belief in immortality. But as we pay our tribute and relive the valued moments that memory recalls, we do something that is equally important. We make our own living a testimony to our belief. We express in our living our concern that the "invincible surmise" of the soul may find in us not an antagonist but one whose faith is equal to the demands of past, present, and future. Such, then, is your mood and purpose on this day. Such, then, is your faith and goal as brothers. I honor you for the impulse that brings you to this service of memorial. I cherish for you the life that can be worthy of a never-ending spiritual privilege.

THEY THAT MOURN

In the Sermon on the Mount, Jesus says something that at first seems contradictory. "Blessed are they that mourn: for they shall be comforted." This is not so much a contradiction as it is a paradox. Often great truth is held in the tension of a paradox. Sorrow and comfort are opposite extremes. Yet wisdom asks us to look closely at sorrow, for in wisely handling our sorrow we find true meaning for life.

Jesus did not say that sorrow was good. He assumed that it was inevitable. It is a part of life, and we do not really begin to live until we learn how to handle sorrow creatively. We can find strength in our sorrow, strange as it may seem.

The word "comfort" means with fortitude, with strength. We cannot know strength without effort. We cannot know comfort until we experienced deprivation. Some persons are destroyed by sorrow. It corrodes their faith, until they are alone with their bitterness and resentment. Others grow strong in facing sorrow with courage. They gain new sensitivity and deep, rich faith. They become more understanding and sympathetic.

86

If we would come to terms with life, we had better discover what it means to cope with sorrow creatively. We are talking now about that inner process by which we become competent in using our grief to heal rather than hurt, to build rather than tear down.

How can you develop this wise approach to your sorrow?

To begin with, you must know that sorrow can bring perspective to life. Life is a combination of joy and sorrow. As drama reaches its noblest form in tragedy, so life can become sublime when it learns how to master tragedy.

Perspective reveals contrasts. Rembrandt achieved mastery as an artist through his use of shadows. His paintings reflect meaning and insight not through brilliant colors but through the strong use of shadow, which makes the light more important even when used sparingly.

The story is told of a woman who appealed to Buddha to restore her child claimed by death. Buddha sent her away to fetch a bowl of peppers from families that had known no such grief. He promised to minister to her need when she returned with the peppers. When evening came, she returned with an empty bowl and a heart full of understanding.

Grief can reveal new depths within our own beings. We can be aware of sensitivities we had not known before. We can become more deeply sympathetic. If we seek only comfort, we are impoverished. We cannot really know comfort until we have been uncomfortable.

Sorrow can teach us the importance of letting go of what we cannot and should not cling to. We usually grieve for ourselves and our loss. This self-centeredness is an important part of our grief, but it is unwise and unrealistic to cling to a past that is already gone. Such an attitude destroys the present and burdens us as we move into the future. Creative sorrow knows how to let go of the past so that we can find a larger meaning in the future.

If we stop to think of it, we know that our inability to let go is evidence of immature emotion. A child clings to a Teddy bear for security. An adult may cling to illusions but finds no security in them, because his mature faith is geared to reality and not to illusions. Maturity brings strength and security as we learn to deal competently with things as they are. Then the inner life learns how to be master of external circumstance.

Our inner security is a counterpart of that evidence of law and order in the universe that depends on cause-effect relations that are predictable. Our security is, then, not a dream to which we cling in futility but, rather, part of the dependable structure of creation itself, and we feel a part of something so much larger than ourselves that we are never alone again.

Doubt produces fear. Faith creates confidence. The fearful soul dies a thousand deaths, while the brave soul never really dies. The strength of faith is the strength of life.

Mature faith does not believe the unbelievable. Rather, it sets goals that are real and uses the energy of life to realize the things that are hoped for. It does not deny reality. Rather, it develops the resources to deal with life wisely and well. Religious faith does not deny the pain of sorrow. Rather, it eases that pain by fitting it to our strengthened resources for meeting it.

Jesus is sometimes referred to as a man of sorrows and acquainted with grief. He was not giving a vain counsel when he spoke. He had learned through experience that man need not fear life and those things that are incident to it if he has found a basis for faith that cannot be shaken.

Jesus would counsel against a false faith that tries to deny what it cannot accept. Rather, he would have us develop that inner strength that takes life and makes of its raw experience a refined product. For certainly this was what he did with the experience of death and the cross. He made it the symbol of spiritual victory and a life eternal.

PATIENT IN TRIBULATION

If there is one thing we are sure of today, it is that tribulation is more than a word. It is an active experience. And farmers of the ancient world had a device they called a *tribulum*. It was used for threshing wheat. The harvested plants were placed in the threshing device and flailed until the grain was separated from the straw or chaff. One part was useful for food and for sowing the fields. The other was of little use and often thrown away. The *tribulum* gives us the origin of the word tribulation. We see it as an experience that winnows from life its valued parts by a process of separation that may be both painful and rewarding.

St. Paul in that wonderful twelfth chapter of Romans pours out advice and counsel. Part of what he says is "Be patient in tribulation." He assumes that tribulation is not a pleasant experience, that it may be painful, but at the same time it may be a valuable experience, so it is not for us so much to fight against it as it is for us to be patient with it.

But Paul does not stop there. His next phrase is, I think, the key to the matter of dealing creatively with tribulation. He adds, "Be constant in prayer."

90

If we are constantly at prayer, we know at once it is not something we do occasionally. Rather it is something that we are all the time. It is a way of life, a way of looking at life. It can be as the leaven in a loaf, something that permeates all about it in order to bring about changes. The yeast turns the dull dough into a more edible product. The attitude of constant prayer turns the raw material of human experience into something that we are able to digest. How does it do it?

In the first place, prayer is a specialized type of thinking. It is thinking with direction and purpose. The way we think helps to make us the way we are. The things we say to ourselves are more important than the things other people say to us. The ideas we cultivate deep within our beings are determinants of behavior. We tend to become what we dwell on in thought. In this sense, whether we admit it or not, we are constantly in prayer. Yet the tragedy of it is that often the things we think are so negative and undesirable that our praying actually is preying upon our own inner being.

When the disciples wanted to discover the unique quality of Jesus' being, they did not ask him to tell them how to think or how to preach or how to prepare parables. No, they asked him to teach them how to pray. And he instructed them in a series of positive views about life and its relationships. Here we get some useful clues as to what is the nature of this specialized thinking that is continually going on.

It seeks to know and do God's will. One of the easy traps we fall into in thinking is that we confuse our own will with the will of God. Then, instead of working for the coming of God's kingdom within man, we work for our own small purposes. This, of course, leads to frustration and narrowing horizons. If, in our minds continually, we hold the thought of the larger will, we tend to live on the growing edge of life, expanding in our consciousness rather than contracting in our consciousness of self.

Also it seeks to live with a forgiving attitude. When we live with resentment, we increase our sensitivity to hurt and injury. When we live with a forgiving attitude, we grow in understanding and good will. And as Jesus points out, our ability to accept forgiveness is related to our ability to give it. We are all so aware of our shortcomings and our need for forgiveness that it would be doing ourselves a real disservice in relation to God to block off our capacity to receive forgiveness merely because we take an unforgiving attitude toward others.

This prayerful attitude our Master taught takes a further step in warning against the kind of thinking that is tempting. We may believe that thinking is not doing, but certainly they are closely related, for thinking leads to doing. If we think tempting thoughts, we are apt to walk in evil ways. In our praying, then, we would seek to have our minds led away from temptation and the consequent evil. This specialized thinking is not easy. It is a full-time job, demanding inner discipline as well as outer control. But mastery at this art made Jesus what he was, and his disciples knew it.

One of the things that can happen to us when we face the winnowing experience of death and its consequent grief is the hazard of wrong thinking, perverted prayer. We tend to feel pity for ourselves, and no emotion produces less benefit than self-pity. We tend to become critical of others, oversensitive to the things they say and do. We tend to become unforgiving and justify our temptation to think unkind thoughts.

It was to this attitude of mind that St. Paul was speaking, I am quite sure. For in order to move through tribulation with constructive thoughts and feelings, to be truly patient, we must use the full resources of our minds to understand the process in which we are immersed. Tribulation is not pleasant, but it is a part of life. The important thing for us to decide is whether we will come through it with rich grain or useless chaff. We are the only ones who can determine what tribulation will do to us. We can turn it to richer sympathy, deeper insight, disciplined attitudes, truer forgiveness, or we can leap into a pool of self-indulgence, self-pity, and self-destruction.

Whenever we stand in the presence of death, we are aware of our own mortality. This in itself is a form of tribulation. What then goes on within us? Does it lead us to fear, anxiety, and a frenzied fight to get away from the fact of our mortal nature, or does it invite us to new self-awareness, self-discipline, and self-fulfillment? It could move either direction. We determine that. Or we can guarantee the positive outcome of our time of tribulation by being patient in it as we remain constant in prayer.

IT IS NOT YOUR FATHER'S WILL

One of the interesting things about common theological utterance is the confidence with which we label a whole variety of events as surely God's will. Last evening, standing in the funeral home, I heard it said that the tragic circumstances that bring us together today were God's will. I want to take a vigorous dissent. I am sure the person who made the remark was trying to think of something comforting to say, so I am not speaking in individual judgment. Rather I want us to face the implications of an attitude of mind that is too prevalent among us.

This unfortunate habit of expression may well grow from a practice of insurance companies in labeling any catastrophe for which man is not responsible as an act of God. This is a phrase used to cover natural events like floods, earthquakes, hurricanes, and lightning. Such events, beyond the control of men, are so-called as a matter of convenience, but certainly it is not very intelligent to label destructive forces as exclusively an expression of God's will.

Men have long lived in fear of natural events that they

94

could not easily control. But it is also true that much of the progress men have made has grown from a responsible effort to adapt and adjust to these natural events. Our skills in architecture are man's answer to the hazards of the elements. Structural steel is an answer to the fear of earthquakes. Weather forecasting and storm-warning systems provide an opportunity for protection against tornadoes and hurricanes. Medical science is an answer to epidemics and disease. Agriculture is an answer to famine. The wisdom of man is continually at work to meet the impact of natural events that could be destructive.

But to move from that to say that the destructive forces that are the product of man's ignorance, carelessness, and willfulness are also expressions of the will of God is to assume something about the nature of God that ill prepares us to see in his nature the evidences of a wise providence at work to give to his creatures a more abundant life. How then do we resolve this problem, so much before us at a time like this? Can we with openness and honesty cope with the things we call accidents?

Man by his very nature is a limited creature. He is not all-wise or all-discerning. His area of knowledge is surrounded by the fact of his ignorance. But his ignorance is an expression of his freedom to know, to explore, to discover. It is not so much the will of God as the expression of his ignorance that a man will build his house over an earthquake fault. When his free use of his ability to grow in knowledge is employed, he will guard against such error. In many respects our study of seismology is now doing just that. But the will of God appears to be expressed more fully in his overcoming of ignorance than in the consequences of it.

Man's limitation is also shown through his carelessness. He continually does through carelessness those things that he knows he should not do. The fire that is man's useful servant can become destructive through his carelessness. But this, too, is an expression of man's failure rather than God's will.

Perhaps we see most clearly the failure of man in his willfulness, when he deliberately does what he knows is not wise or good. He often does this in relation to himself to jeopardize his health. He does it in relation to the things he can use either wisely and well or with deliberate disdain of law and order. He deliberately runs risks and invites consequences.

But one of the more puzzling aspects of man's ignorance, carelessness, and willfulness is the circumstance of the innocent suffering for the shortcomings of others. No man lives entirely unto himself. We are all bound together in the processes of living in a complex society. Often this produces an event in which the chain reaction of human behavior engulfs those who are not personally responsible, but share the results of a collective responsibility from which we cannot easily escape.

In war we see the breakdown of normal human relationships, through which hardship is worked upon the innocent and helpless. The National Safety Council tells us that most persons killed in highway accidents are not guilty of breaking the rules of the road but suffer the results of others' lawlessness. Man's inhumanity to man continues to take its toll, and we all to a greater or lesser extent bear the burden in consequence.

Our richest resource, in trying to face the consequences of such misfortune, is the belief that the universe is on the side of order, wisdom, and justice, and that the nature of God would lead man, through the use of his freedom, toward that moral consciousness that would right wrongs rather than compound them.

We can see how important it is for us not to confuse the nature of God's ultimate will with the failures of men. To assume that God is a murderer, an arsonist, a careless destroyer of what he has made removes us from the faith and comfort we need most at the time it is essential for our balanced thought and action.

Heavy as the burden of human responsibility may be for us, it is better to assume it individually and collectively than to pollute the wellsprings of spiritual support. Today of all days it is clearly our necessity to make sure that we know in our minds and spirits that those things that so deeply distress us are the evidence of man's violation of God's will rather than the manifestation of it.

Only as we face the facts of human frailty and failure with openness and honesty are we able to accept the responsibilities for the changes that must be made so that man can cope more adequately with these evidences of his limitation. But we come together not in our despair to make God responsible for the failures of men. Rather, we stand humbly before God with the sure knowledge that his will is on the side of wisdom, righteousness, and truth. When we accept our obligations to limit and relieve man's igorance, carelessness, and willfulness, we are working with God to help his will become a way of life. As long as we are finite beings, we will be aware of our shortcomings, but woe to us if we try to blame God for the individual and collective abuse of our freedom.

FULL SPIRITUAL STATURE

In the presence of physical death we are obliged to stand tall, to assert our right to stand at our full spiritual stature. Often in the presence of the unknown or the distressing, we are apt to cower or cringe. This puts us at a disadvantage, for we then are not able to meet the onslaughts of circumstance with fullness of spirit but rather accept the mood of defeat before we face the facts.

Each one of us today brings to this moment a variety of thought, feelings, and experience that have come from our own pathway of life. If the past has been uncertain, we are apt to be uncertain and off balance. If the past has been secure and good, we bring that strength and confidence into this moment. And it is inevitable that what happens during this time together will become part of the equipment with which we face the future, whether it be to our liking or not.

If we can find the inner resources to stand tall in the presence of death, we may go from this sanctuary fortified for any other event that has the mark of death upon it. How can we learn to stand tall?

The story is told of a lonely traveler in Alaska who was traveling a trail that was new to him. He proceeded with caution. When he came to a river, he was not certain of the thickness of the ice, so he lay down on the ice and with care and apprehension half-crawled and half-slid across the river. Exhausted from his efforts, he climbed up on the other bank to rest and catch his breath. While sitting there, he heard a noise in the distance and soon recognized it as a motor. In a few minutes a large truck loaded with many tons of logs came into sight. It was driving down the center of the river, using the ice as a highway. Where a few moments before he had been crawling in fear, the truck was now proceeding with confidence.

There are times when in meeting new life experiences we crawl in apprehension when we could with confidence stand at our full spiritual stature. Often when we come face to face with death, with its unknown and unknowable aspects, we try to deny the fact or shrink away from it in assumed littleness. This attitude is not good enough.

What then can we do? How can we assume a stance that is in violation of our inner feelings?

Your questions are well put. We need first to face our feelings of apprehension and dismay. One of the things that makes man unique is that he can stand off and look at the nature of life. He can measure it in space and time, because he has not only the capacity to measure life but also the capacity to understand the meaning of his death. This is the source of much of his anxiety. But it can also be the source of his faith, and this faith is the answer to his anxiety. It is his ability to be aware of something within himself that is not subject to space and time. This is the root of his belief in immortality. If he were not aware of one, he could not be aware of the other.

Man's awareness of his spiritual nature gives to his living, even while it is bound by space and time, a freedom from these limitations. He knows he is not made for death alone, otherwise he would not struggle so to know its meaning. The history of religion is the expression of man's effort to come to terms with his capacity for God-consciousness, which in its very essence removes his contemplation from the merely time bound. His quest for the meaning of his existence frames it within those concepts that are infinite and eternal. So in life he is aware of what is already beyond life, physically speaking.

Our Christian faith gives to us in abundant measure the assurance that life is more than biology, more than a personal history that flickers for a time and then is no more. The meaning for life is already an extension of that life beyond mere biology and history.

We begin to understand the fuller meaning of the revelation of our Lord when we sense that his use of space and time for a while was an indication of that sublime quality in man that is able to use the measurable to reveal the immeasurable.

Modern science has made it clear to us that space and time are relative and merely the devices man has made for interpreting the experience of life. But the quality of life is not limited by some of its measurements, any more than a yard of cloth is nothing but the yardstick by which it is measured.

It is here that we begin to see that even biology can be a clue to what is beyond it. Just as our lungs have no meaning apart from the air they breathe, and our eyes have no meaning apart from the light they use, and our ears have no meaning apart from the sounds they hear, so the soul of man has no meaning apart from the spiritual nature to which it is attuned.

We see then that our anxiety about death is an expression of our preoccupation with the measurable, the physical. But we are not made for that alone. Something important within us is craving to exist beyond measurement, beyond space and time. The meaning of this something else makes it possible for us to look at death and not be confounded by it, to measure life and yet not be lost in our measurements.

When we are able to come to a moment such as this with the very present evidences of man's limited nature biologically, but firmly believe that his nature is more than biology and those things so incident to this limited nature, we begin to see what is meant when we hear those words, "Death is swallowed up in victory." Our faith speaks of the victory of spiritual meaning over biological events.

When we measure life by that faith and that meaning, we need no longer be overcome by our anxiety, but rather we can stand tall, to our full stature as spiritual beings. For our ability to measure is a clue to our ability to sense the measureless. Our capacity to know time is our assurance of eternity. Our awareness of space is our clue to the infinite. These higher sensitivities, this awareness of the infinite and eternal is the very stuff of which our spiritual nature is made. In this we glory for it marks us as unique, spiritual beings for a period tasting of space and time, but only because our true nature is at home in the infinite and the eternal. So stand tall. It is your birthright. So also, it is your death right.

FAITH FOR LIFE'S CRISES

Life is not made to move with calmness and undisturbed quiet through all our years. There are days of stress and crisis when the things that happen cause us deep distress. No journey, it seems, is without its storms and no life without its times of testing. But that is not a circumstance without its blessings, for only in times of stress can we find the deeper meaning of the faith that sustains us in living and in the presence of death.

The faith we affirm is not a generalized faith. It speaks to life's specific needs. There is really no generalized death either, for the only death we really know is the specific death that diminishes the circle of those with whom we have lived and sought life's meaning. Today we would seek to understand how our specific faith helps us deal with the specific crises that life brings with it.

There are certain ingredients of our faith. High on the list of these ingredients is the willingness to look honestly at things as they are. Our faith is geared to reality, not to fancy. But there are times when it is more difficult to see things clearly than at others. I remember once wandering through the bazaar in Cairo where there were many small factories. The artisans were at work plying their varied trades. I stopped at a place where children were at work making rugs. I stood for a while watching with fascination at the almost mechanical movement of these youngsters. But I was baffled by the results, because the product of their efforts seemed to be a meaningless jumble of color and inept design. Evidently the supervisor noted my puzzled expression for he came over and said, "Come on this side to see the pattern." Sure enough, when he tilted up the loom so I could see the other side, the pattern was clear and the color a beautiful blend of complementing shades.

There are times in life when things do not make sense and when the pattern and design is lost in our pain and suffering. It is then that our faith says to us that there is another side if we can but see it, and what is beyond our ken may well make sense when we perceive quite a different thing.

Our faith also gives us the strength to move beyond the known into the unknown with confidence. It is reported that the generals of Alexander the Great were distressed when their emperor urged them on into the unknown. They remonstrated saying, "But we are marching off the map." But under his command they kept on going and discovered the Himalayas. There are times when we become apprehensive in new circumstances and say, "But we never did that before. We never thought that before. We never believed that before." Fine. That shows that you are on the growing edge of life. Nothing stifles life like living in a cozy little world bounded by our past experience. We need to think courageously and act daringly to be worthy of new opportunities in life. Fear can paralyze life while faith can give you the courage to march off the map.

Death is a great unknown. It is often looked at as one of the boundaries of life. But the difference between a boundary and a frontier is that we tend to be stopped by one and urged on by the other. Our faith makes death a frontier, not a boundary; not an end, but a new beginning.

Our faith also gives us the power to take off into realms of meaning that do not exist apart from faith. I well remember years ago when flying was primitive. The plane bumped along on crude runways until we almost despaired of getting off, and then finally the bumping stopped, and we knew we were airborne. But it was uncertain because the power sources were limited. Now the thundering power of jet engines smoothly thrusts us across the runway and with a daring display of power flaunts gravity as the plane steeply ascends into the sky. The difference is the power available.

The nature of our faith determines whether we are bumping along with dread and uncertainty, or whether we are meeting the crises of life by drawing on reserves of spiritual energy that make it possible for us to soar above them. This faith is rooted in the belief that the universe is on the side of our highest aspirations and that we rise in strength when we let the power of God live in and through us.

Emerson wrote, "Hold a straw parallel to the Gulf Stream, and the Atlantic Ocean will flow through it." Hold your life parallel to God's will, and the creative power of the universe will flow through it. But deny or resist that will and life is buffeted as a straw in a storm.

This faith is not an accident in human experience. It is an achievement of daring thinking and courageous action. The thinking has prepared the way for the action, and the action once completed is so self-verifying that it enriches the faith. Together they strengthen and enrich life, so that it takes the crises and uses them for creative purposes, rather than becoming the helpless straw in the hands of a cruel fate.

If, in the midst of these circumstances that bring us together today, we find a new assurance and determination to think of the meaning of our lives as they relate to the revelation of God's power and wisdom at work in the universe, this may well be for us a time of new beginnings, worthier impulses, and nobler goals. For even the storms may drive us more rapidly toward the goal. And the facing of death may be for us a time when we face the meaning and purpose of life with new discernment.

HOW TO ACHIEVE SERENITY

Anxiety is the compounded fear that grows from having to face the things we cannot do anything about. Or at least that is what we are apt to think. But our religious faith tells us that we can do something about the most distressing things, perhaps not externally but surely internally. Today when we are face to face with physical things that we cannot do anything about, it is doubly important for us to make sure of that inner domain, where we can stay in control and surely do something to bring relief.

Jesus told his hearers, "Be not anxious." He had pointed out that a material preoccupation with barns full of grain could not nourish a soul that was faced with the full meaning of life and death. A faith that believes that underneath life there is a power to sustain its best aspirations is affirmed by looking at the beauty of a lily or the self-confidence of a bird. The fact of faith is that God sustains life and that the life that lives in that faith does not need to become anxious about material things, for they are incidental. Death, as we observe it now, is material and so incidental. The spirit's life is nonmaterial, and so it is beyond the physical events that bring us together today.

Our concern is to seek first the kingdom of God and his righteousness. Then all other things will take their right relationship. An ancient prayer puts the matter in proper perspective. It says, "God, give me the serenity to accept what cannot be changed, and the courage to change what can be changed, and the wisdom to know one from the other."

There is wisdom in the serenity to accept. No one can add by his effort an inch to his height or change the color of his eyes or significantly modify many other aspects of his inheritance. He must accept himself as he is in these respects as a starting point for life. Yet we have all known persons who were so deeply distressed by some trifling aspect of their nature or appearance that they denied or put at serious disadvantage all the rest of their living.

Also we have observed those people who spend most of their time so worked up about things they cannot do anything about that they have no interest, time, or energy left for the things they could modify. We cannot do anything about the death that has happened, but we can do something about the life that is happening now and will continue to live tomorrow and next month and next year. The serenity to accept what cannot be changed is not only common sense but is highly economical of energy and human resources.

But equally important is the courage to change what can be changed and what should not be accepted. The frustration and anxiety that is produced by trying to do the impossible is quite different from the satisfaction and reward one feels in doing what makes sense and is essentially useful. The place to start, of course, is with ourselves. How much energy is used up in fuming and stewing, which could more effectively be used to change the very conditions that distress us. How often we become so overwhelmed by self-pity and excessive and inappropriate emotion that we miss the opportunities lying close at hand to help others and give to our own living a sense of satisfaction.

Let us not deceive ourselves, for even in death there is much that can be changed, that needs to be changed. To begin with, our own attitude toward death needs to be examined to see where it falls short of the Christian ideal. Then we can move beyond ourselves to see how we, as part of a healing, redeeming community, can minister to human need so that the weak are strengthened, the foolish made wiser, and the separated brought into the fold of human concern. Surely there is much to be done that we are in a position to do if we are courageous and discerning.

But the nub of the matter comes in gaining the wisdom to know one from the other. Sometimes we are serene and placid in the midst of injustice and human suffering. Sometimes we are courageous without wisdom and go riding off on crusades that are lacking in prudence and that function without facts. The wisdom that can sort out the experience of life into the acceptable and unacceptable is not achieved at once but is the product of long and careful study and prayerful contemplation. It grows from a concern about the spiritual values that makes sure that material things are always considered as means and the things that affect the lives of persons deeply are the ends. Perhaps, as Jesus pointed out with the man and his barns, there is nothing that does so much to make us aware of the difference between means and ends as the fact of death itself.

Certainly it is at a time like this that we are faced most specifically with that question, "Are we barn builders or soul builders?"

Our anxiety grows from our preoccupation with the things we know we cannot take with us. Our serenity increases when we feel sure that the values we live by have the right to survive that event related to material things that we call death.

Too often we seek to allay our anxieties by resort to sedatives and tranquilizers. These devices, however, can delude us into thinking we have found a serenity which is in effect only a postponement of our facing of reality. The serenity we speak of today is not sedation or escape. Rather it is a claim upon the full power of our faith that is adequate for both life and death. When we seek first the kingdom of God and his righteousness, we organize our living quest around exalted goals, we build up treasure beyond moth, rust, or corrosion. Then our whole being responds with the serenity of knowing that our investment is in eternal things.

It might be well for us, not only today when we are mindful of death, but every day when we would be mindful of the fullest meaning of life, that we should say,

"God, give me serenity to accept what cannot be changed,
And courage to change what can be changed,
And the wisdom to know one from the other."

ON LEARNING HOW TO FORGET

That may seem to you to be an inappropriate theme for our thought together today when our minds are so stabbed awake with a flood of memories. And I would not want to say anything to deny you the richness of memory. However, we know quite well that memory is a selective process. The right use of memory can enrich and fulfill life. The wrong use of memory can burden and enslave life, until it seems we cannot carry the load of torturing memories. How then can we make memory a privilege rather than a problem?

St. Paul gives us a clue. He wrote, "Forgetting what lies behind and straining forward to what lies ahead, I press on toward the goal for the prize of the upward call of God in Christ Jesus." Certainly St. Paul had known tragedy, suffering, bereavement, and the burden of death. He was probably speaking to himself as much as to the members of the church at Philippi and to us here today. What was the burden of his message?

If we work at it, we can hold on to things of the past that we should gladly let go of. A psychologist writes, "It is the

110

function of the brain to enable us not to remember but to forget." Our bodies cannot recall pain, they can only recall some of the thoughts or feelings that accompany it. That is why we so easily speak of forgotten pains. The cumulative burden of suffering, anxiety, and fear in life would be impossible to bear were not the mind skilled at the task of selectively dropping from memory those things that are intolerable.

But there are times when we make it difficult for our minds to perform their appointed tasks. We exert powerful energy to hold on to what should be let go of. We immerse ourselves in self-pity and self-torture. In doing this we create an unreal world and try to live in it. We know that we cannot live in the past, but often we try to do it. What we actually do is to put the present in jeopardy by trying to reorient our existence in terms of what it has come from rather than what it is going toward. So we can carry the fears, the failures, the enmities, and the grudges of the past into the present and the future. We can use the powerful emotions that are generated at the time of death to fortify our grasp on the past, rather than to accept the invitation of the future.

St. Paul knew what he was talking about. For years he had been a most vigorous enemy of Christendom. He had used the power of his mind and the influence of his position to embarrass, injure, brutalize, and destroy individual Christians and the organized movement. He was fervently mistaken, and then one day he saw the light and made a complete turnabout. At first those whom he had persecuted did not know whether they should trust him or not, but in time he proved himself. Yet, if he had carried his burden of guilt into every new situation, he would have been severely handicapped. He knew that. He wanted to preserve the power of his incentive but at the same time free himself from the burdens which the past would have placed on him. He wanted to work effectively in the present with his eyes on the future rather than looking always over his shoulder at the shortcomings of the past.

Whenever we are faced with death, we have as part of our response that feeling that we express in various ways. You have heard it many times when people say, "If only I had known," or, "If I had it to do over again." When we are completely honest with ourselves, we all know that we could have done better. But there is one thing we are also sure of and that is that we cannot turn the clock back, we cannot live by last year's calendar, we cannot retreat into the unreality of living in a past that is gone. If our life is to have vitality and meaning, it will take what it has wisely learned of the past and put it to work in the present and the future.

It was this concern for the present and future that St. Paul focused his mind on. "I press on toward the goal" is in the present tense. The prize is granted in the future as the result of the efforts that are made as the present opportunity is used. He was working at the important task of selectively forgetting so that he could do his best work for the kingdom.

Sometimes in small communities this is a difficult task. The accumulation of things and people who remind us of the past are ever present. Really we would not want it otherwise, for there is a difference between ignoring and forgetting. In one way our minds never forget, for everything that has ever happened to us is stored up in our various levels of consciousness but usually out of memory or recall. The other part of our mind is at work consciously to control what we keep in the focus of our attention. We remember something by forgetting something else. We forget what is not worth remembering by directing our thought toward what is worthy of the mark of our high calling.

Like everything else in life, our memories need to be dedicated to the use of our Christian conviction about life. If we are the sensitive type of person who says it is hard to forget some things, we are merely saying that we have a harder task to perform to be worthy of our Christian inheritance. The abuse of our minds, to keep warmed up the things we should long since have forgotten, can hatch out a swarm of life-infecting creatures that we have little need of. How often we hear reference to this costly practice —like the man who denies himself the benefit of religion because of something that happened in the church twenty years ago, or the person who will not forget a slight or an old misunderstanding. It is a misuse of our ability to forget to remember other people's mistakes while we forget our own. It is a distortion of normal living to cling to painful memories when we could find easy release by selective and purposeful forgetting.

When we come face to face with the ultimates of life and death, many of the other things of life seem trivial and unimportant. Perhaps this is the place and time for each of us to take a fresh look at the admonition of St. Paul. He was talking sense. He was offering himself and you a future freed of the burdens of unwise memory and unfruitful recrimination. In its stead he was inviting a dedication of our mental processes to the high calling of God in Jesus Christ and the reward of life it offers us.

THE WAY EVERLASTING

The ways of life are tenuous at best. Man stands always close to the threshold of the mystery of death. The functioning of a small but tough muscle that pumps our blood marks the boundary that separates this known from the unknown. Records show that disease of the heart is the number one cause of death today. This makes the lines of the Psalmist sung centuries before the Christian era strangely relevant for us:

> Search me, O God, and know my heart!
> Try me and know my thoughts!
> And see if there be any wicked way in me,
> and lead me in the way everlasting!

The Psalmist was well aware of the double meaning of the heart, for it is not only an essential piece of pumping equipment. It is also so sensitive to our emotions that in common language the heart is accepted as the center of our emotional life. The Psalmist knew that right thinking must be matched with right feeling if life is to achieve an eternal quality while yet in time.

114

The Psalmist used quaint but graphic phrases to describe the burden of grief felt by the heart. He spoke of it being melted like wax or being poured out within. We can probably attest from our own experience to feelings comparable to these. When the Scripture speaks of the heart disquieted within, we get a clue to the meaning of the phrase, "Keep thy heart with all diligence."

The importance of properly keeping the heart is affirmed by the researches of medicine. It is pointed out that accumulated fear, worry, and tension put an added burden on this instrument so sensitive to our feelings, and in truth, "from it flow the springs of life."

The New Testament speaks to this concern of the heart. "Let not your heart be troubled, neither let it be afraid." But the advice does not stop there. It is not a counsel of perfection unrelated to our need or experience. It is an expression of basic wisdom supported even now by the latest research of the scientist.

How does one keep his heart with diligence so that the important issues of life are settled with right feeling and right action? Those who study the response of the heart claim that it is constricted by hate, fear, jealousy, bitterness, and resentment. These feelings so constrain life that the inner parts are not able to separate themselves from the strain. The release of life from these destructive emotions comes when we are able to learn how to respond to the opposites—love, faith, acceptance, understanding, and good will. From the most practical point of view, we cannot afford destructive feelings, for they take too much out of us. We cannot afford not to open our lives to creative feelings, for they are a guarantee of a right condition within. It is said that John Wesley and the other members of the early Wesleyan revival movement had a special greeting

with which they saluted each other when they met. It was
"Is your heart right?" Instead of a mere "Good day" or
"How are you?" they put their finger on the central issue
of life, the point where feelings are generated, and asked in
effect if they were harboring right feelings within.

There is a strange parallel between the Wesleyans and
the words of the Psalmist. He would open himself to God
to see if deep within his innermost being, at the seat of his
thought and feeling, he was holding any wicked attitudes.
He knew that if this were so, it would poison his whole
being and stand in the way of his achievement of his right
relationship with God. The path along the way everlasting
was not trod with the burdens of destructive feelings. The
heart must be opened to God's scrutiny, so that thought and
feeling are worthy.

What the insight of the Scriptures made known centuries
ago is finding abundant verification in the studies of our
medical scientists. Illness is seen more and more to be a
type of organic behavior, an acting out in the total being
of attitudes and feelings that possess us. In fact at one of the
major diagnostic clinics in this country, they have worked
out correlations of emotional states with certain types of
disease that they can predict with amazing accuracy.

Grief is a powerful feeling. It can set at work in the core
of our beings emotional states that we hardly knew existed
within us. Our grief may open channels for the outflow of
emotions that run back to the earliest years of life and that
have seemed to be dormant for years. Our grief can make
us oversensitive to misunderstanding and overwrought in our
expressions. Surely this is a time for special consideration
for the feelings of others and a special diligence in guarding
our own hearts.

How shall we do this? First by recognizing the special needs that we have in times of great emotional stress. We have to be especially kind to our hearts, our friends, and those others who share the time of stress with us.

We also need to recognize the spiritual resources that are available for us at these times. Often I hear persons say, "I didn't know that I had such strength in me." They meet major crises better than they meet minor ones. And there is good reason, for in little things they go it alone, but in the big things they know their limitations and are willing to call upon the spiritual reserves God will make available to those who open their hearts to his searching ways without restraint or false pride.

God never places upon us more than we can endure, but that is not to say that those who foolishly try to meet stress without help are going to be untouched by it. Rather, the time of extra burden is the time when, with openness of heart, we can seek God's presence and help. Never do we feel more aware of the vulnerable nature of our mortal state than when we stand in the presence of death and feel overwhelmed by the feelings of grief. But if we are to do the work of mourning well, we seek to free ourselves of the thoughts and feelings that might poison the wellsprings of life, and open our minds and spirits that they may be possessed by the presence and the power of God, for surely this is the best way to be led "in the way everlasting."

THE ETERNAL QUESTION

We are met in the quietness of this solemn hour to pay our final tribute as a group to the life of a man. He walked among us in friendliness and good will for his allotted span of years, and then quietly, as he had lived, he took his departure. We are faced with some basic questions as we meet here. What is the meaning of a life like his? Like a flower of the field it springeth up and flourisheth, and then it is no more. What does it all mean? In effect we are asking that ancient question, "What is man, that thou art mindful of him?"

In quiet moments of contemplation as well as in times of acute stress this question of meaning comes to us. What is life all about? What am I? Why have I been put here?

The Psalmist asked the question in one form, and Job in another. Plato, St. Thomas Aquinas, Copernicus, and Darwin asked the question in different ways but always with the same import.

The answer to the question is important, for our answer carries the central element of our philosophy of life. Is man a complicated animal? If nothing more than that, he takes his place with the lower forms of life that crawl the planet. Is man a person? What is the special quality of his personality that separates him from all other creatures that are compounded of what they are and do? Is man a sample of the universe, finding his meaning in the revelation of a meaning that is charged with purpose, design, and direction? If so, he is not separated from, but is a part of, a self-conscious cosmic purpose at work to unfold itself in creation. Or is man a servant of God? A creature who is not important to God for his value but is essential to God's purpose in his fulfillment of freedom?

We have long since learned that a physical thing is equal to the sum of its parts. But with man it is different, for he is always something more than the sum of his parts. If we take him apart to find this elusive element, it escapes us. If we try to explain him without it, our explanations are not adequate.

And just when we think that we have come to the place where we have found a good enough answer, we discover more things about man that send us back to our task of seeking answers that are big enough to cover all we observe and experience. For the problem with man is that he is self-conscious and God-conscious. He uses his mind, a part of himself, to try to explain these capacities of consciousness, and he never comes up with a big enough theory to encompass all there is to man.

The more we cope with this baffling question, the more we sense something quite irrational and yet inescapable— that man achieves a stature in his own eyes comparable to what he measures himself by. If he thinks he is just an animal, he tends to become nothing more than an animal. If he thinks he is a partner of God in a cosmic enterprise, he becomes a little less than the angels.

Man is essentially a value creator. The essential nature of his worship is to stand in awe before a creator of supreme values. When Jesus said, "I and the father are one," he was making the most daring kind of affirmation about the nature of man. He was stating the mystical union that exists between creature and creator. When we look to the revelation of Jesus, we set the measure by which all men may ultimately be measured. When Pilate said, "Behold the man," he little realized the grandeur of his utterance.

When Jesus stood before Pilate, he was deserted and alone. By the end of the century there were thousands of Christians; by the third century, half a million; and by the sixth century, fifteen million. Today half a billion persons look to that revelation as the ultimate answer to the question, "What is man?" For in Jesus, the Christ, the ultimate of values becomes a living fact. Today those values for the nature of man are still the measure. We do not say, "Behold the church," for we are too conscious of its imperfections; but we continue to say, "Behold the Man," for we know that no one on earth can live as if that ultimate measurement for life had not been made.

Yes, ask the question at a low level and get a low answer. Ask it at a high level, and we come face to face with the high-water mark of human experience, and are forced to measure ourselves by the highest we know.

The Psalmist asked the question as if he thought God was doing man a favor to be mindful of him. Jesus, in his affirmation of a vital and living unity between creature and creator, set the base for a partnership in comprehending things divine. We keep discovering new things about the mind and spirit of man. We keep growing in our awareness of the meaning of man's dominion, but the ultimate of that dominion is an awareness that makes him humbly great and greatly humble at the same time. Within his being he has the resource to become one with God in the processes of creation and fulfillment within that part of life and experience that is his. He has great powers to lay waste or to create. He cannot escape a partnership with God. He can only determine what he will do with that partnership, whether he will be worthy of it or not. Jesus, the Christ, showed that the possibility and the realization become one in revelation. Man has never been able to be the same since that time. He has never been able to be fully satisfied with the lesser answers since that time.

Fortunately, the answer is found in a process, an emerging series of events in history, for the Holy Spirit is alive and at work within us. Each time we see a man taste of death, we sense that greater dimension of his nature as he shares in a partnership that knows no smallness of relationship, for it is revealed in the ultimate answer to the ancient question. Man and God share a common creative capacity. They share the marks of values that are eternal. When Jesus said, "I and the father am one," he was claiming for himself, and potentially for all mankind, the most audacious answer to the ancient question. No one can live again as if that answer had not been made.

YOUR CHURCH AND THE EXPERIENCE OF DEATH

As we are well aware today, one of the basic adjustments we have to make in life sooner or later is to the fact of death. Death is a part of life and we see it in the experience of friends and loved ones, and ultimately in ourselves.

Some persons cannot face this fact satisfactorily and their lives are permanently disrupted by it. They become embittered and disillusioned about the goodness of life. Others adjust to the fact of death and deepen the meaning of life through making the necessary adjustments. They become more understanding and mellowed by it.

The Christian's faith should be an important factor in determining the way he accepts this fact. In the first place the Christian does not think that all of life is physical. He does not see final defeat in the cessation of the physical part of existence for he knows that man has a "physical body and a spiritual body." While they are bound together during the phase of physical existence, they are not ended

122

at the same time, and the spiritual being has an existence beyond space and time.

Strengthened by that faith, the Christian can meet death honestly and without illusion. When the death is the culmination of a long and useful life, he sees it as a part of God's wise plan for life. The life of man shares the characteristics of all of the rest of nature physically. He wears out and returns to the elements of the earth from whence he came. Then the Christian is thankful for the life that is completed, and although he may be personally lonely, he is not moved to condemn the process of life of which physical death is but one part.

When death is tragic and comes before the term of life has been lived to its conclusion, the problems of adjustment may be more difficult. The problem of injustice, the waste of human resources, and the possibility of the innocent suffering for the guilty have to be considered. This places heavier demands on one's philosophy of life and adds stress to the process of adjustment.

When the Christian faces tragedy, his faith sustains him for it has a cross at the center. The cross is the symbol of spiritual victory over the fact of sin and injustice. In order to achieve spiritual fulfillment in life it is often necessary to face the testing of circumstance. Although this may not be the reason for tragedy, it can be the end toward which it is employed.

The Christian church serves the grief-stricken person in two important ways. It furnishes the outline of a philosophy of life that can meet the most tragic conditions, and it gives the framework within which the acute emotional stress of grief can be worked through healthfully.

The Christian faith is a revelation which is supported by the most careful scientific and experiential examination of life. This revelation was made explicit in the life of Jesus, who faced death with the courage of one who knew death was not an end but a beginning. Man's spiritual inheritance from God is of so great value that it could not be wiped out as meaningless. It was St. Paul who made the logic of this inheritance specific when he said that "we are children of God, and if children, then heirs, heirs of God and fellow heirs with Christ, provided we suffer with him in order that we may also be glorified with him."

It is the Christian's faith that his spiritual heritage is not a cosmic accident but rather a product of God's design. So man is prepared for a spiritual existence, and this preparation involves not only the basic capacity for a spiritual life but also a responsibility for the nurture of it. For this spiritual nature is a seed or spark of consciousness within that can be developed to tremendous proportions by disciplined effort. This is perhaps the richer meaning of the parables of growth that Jesus used in referring to the inner kingdom as a mustard seed, a grain of wheat, or a fruitful tree. If God made us to grow into our full stature as spiritual beings, we may be sure that those accidents so incident to our finite nature cannot frustrate or deny the ultimate will of God. Our belief in justice and God's goodness is not dependent upon the interpretation of some incident of our physical existence, but rather upon our acceptance of the revelation of God's infinite power and wisdom through the triumph of Christ over death itself.

The church also furnishes the surroundings through which the strong emotions that accompany grief may find healthful expression. There is no known way of removing the pain and suffering that accompany acute grief. The use of tranquilizers and sedatives merely postpones the inevitable and tends to make the delayed reactions more difficult to cope with. The pain of grief is a healthy and normal thing, and can be dealt with well within the bounds of normal, healthy behavior.

The church helps to do this by encouraging a realistic facing of the fact of death. Illusion is damaging, and a false approach to reality cripples life itself. Physical death is a fact and it must be faced with all of the loneliness, separation, and discomfort that it involves. The church helps its members to accept the physical reality of death through the honest words of the funeral service and the prayers that surround the actual interring of the physical remains. This is the fact of life, and although it is painful, the church shares your pain to the bitter end but it does not recognize that the bitter end is the only end, for the gloom of Good Friday has its Easter, the tomb is subject to a resurrection, and the promise of God is a life that is eternal.

The church encourages its people to express all of the feelings they genuinely feel. Modern medicine verifies the fact that suppressed feelings often become the basis of delayed physical symptoms. Often ulcerative colitis, arthritis, diabetes, and even cancer can be traced to unresolved grief. The free and frank expression of all the feelings, at the time they are felt, relieves the inner stress and helps to prevent the delayed symptoms that can result from the grief that is not properly worked through.

The process of mourning is recognized by the religious community as a normal and legitimate process. It does not deny a basic faith, but it does recognize the depth of human emotion that needs to be expressed. So the church, through its ministry and its fellowship, sustains and supports its bereaved members at the same time that it is quietly and firmly demanding that the physical reality of death be honestly faced.

One of the important things that the church does for its bereaved is to guarantee a way of life that looks toward the future. So often when an important person in one's life dies, the bereft may feel that this is the end of useful life for him, also. The church engages such a person in group activities so that he feels the ongoing motion of life itself and is gradually brought to the place where his life finds a new usefulness and a new interest. Working, worshiping, singing, and praying together strengthen life and support the individual who is going through the difficult adjustment that bereavement brings.

The church, as the custodian of a way of life, is important for a person not only at the crises of life but also at those important times of preparation. The resources to meet stress can be built up through a long and slow process of meditation and worship. Inner strength can be developed through the study of the Scriptures and those other devotional books that help to enrich the inner spiritual life. Then the words that are spoken in times of stress have a depth of meaning that gives added significance to them.

The church, through its sacraments and through its other acts of worship, brings strength, comfort, and enrichment to life. While there is no easy way to face severe loss, there are ways to help the person to grow in understanding and inner power. This is what Jesus meant when he uttered that Beatitude, "Blessed are they that mourn: for they shall be comforted." Death is inevitable, but those who learn to face it with courage and an interpretation that is rooted in spiritual values find a comfort that not only meets their immediate need but also builds into life a richer understanding and a finer sympathy for all others who suffer.

The Christian faces death honestly, bravely, and with a determination to grow through the experience toward that way of life that is strengthened through testing and fulfilled in the practice of a daring faith in the promises of God revealed through the life and teaching of Jesus, the Christ.

PART III

EDUCATION TO MEET LIFE AND DEATH

During recent years I have spoken to many thousands of clergymen about the pastoral care of persons in crisis. Often the discussion centered on the church's role in meeting the needs of the grief-stricken. Question was often raised about ways in which the total program of the church could be strengthened, so that people would be better prepared to use the resources of faith to meet the stresses of life.

Certainly one of the answers that would be given is that the educational, doctrinal, and inspirational opportunities afforded by preaching could be used more extensively to that end. If the preaching program for the year includes sermons that focus attention on the relation of life to death and on the spiritual qualities of man's nature, these become basic insights that persons will fall back on when they are faced with the clear evidences of mortality.

The church calendar affords strategic days for this emphasis. Easter is the focal point of the spiritual victory over physical death. Other days throughout the year give an opportunity for both a direct and an indirect approach to the subject.

With this matter of preaching to a whole philosophy of life, a way of looking at life that is not afraid to consider any of the aspects of man's personal history, we naturally ask, "How can we get beyond theory and see how it may be done?"

Because preaching is essentially an art form, a unique type of utterance that is part of a service of worship, the varied usage would be dependent upon the personalities of those who employ the medium of communication. This is as it should be, for it is not a matter of deciding whether there are right and wrong ways of doing it, but rather what is the right way for the particular preacher. Even here there may be many right ways, depending on circumstances and inspirations.

In the five sermons that follow different objectives are set and differing methods used. They are presented because they may indicate the range of subject matter and the possibilities of both a direct and indirect method of approach.

In "The Eternal Prelude" we have the sermon that is clearly designed to use the historical event of Easter and the prevalent mood of the day to open the door toward the deeper considerations of the meaning of life and death. The emphasis is placed on the developing of values that have a right to survive.

In "The Via Dolorosa—A Way of Mastery over Suffering" the sermon is used to take a bold look at the causes of suffering and man's responsibility in relation to the suffering. It does not center on grief as a form of suffering, but grief is the emotion implicit in the text and the development of the ideas.

In "The Choice Is Ours" the meaning of freedom as the basic element of our responsibility is interpreted. Here the sermon educates the hearers about the need for an adequate philosophy of life, and the inspiration of religion is used to stimulate the thinking necessary for such a philosophy of wholeness.

In "The Belief in Life That Does Not End" the sermon is used to marshal and organize the basic thinking of the religious and philosophical mind about the nature of immortality and the way of life that is worthy of achieving endlessness. The fact that it is more philosophical than mystical is part of the design to keep it closely geared to reality and rational thinking, for often in such matters people's thinking is subservient to their emotions and does not relate them to reality as much as to a world of fancy and wishful thinking. Because the religious faith is most effectively expressed in relation to reality rather than to fancy, it is important to make this emphasis quite often.

Because the nature of the spiritual life is apt to be inundated by the materialistic considerations of our day, it is basic that this nature of the spiritual life be presented in any way that can catch the imagination and fancy of the hearers. In the sermon "The Indwelling Spirit" the whole sermon is built around an analogy. Homiletically this is hazardous procedure, but in actual practice it seemed to work satisfactorily, partly because of personal reference and group identification. It is an indication of how the spiritual quality of life can be lifted up before a congregation, so that indirectly the philosophy of wholeness can be strengthened.

Often the feeling is expressed that people don't want sermons of this type and so the pastor is doubly distressed in preaching them: because he doesn't really want to and because he feels his people don't want him to. Underlying this feeling is a far more general mood of a death-denying, death-defying cultural atmosphere. It is easier in our day to joke about death or to try to ignore it than to face the fact that man is a mortal creature. Perhaps his religion is the last stronghold of an honest facing of both life and death. So the tasks that may at times seem difficult may well be doubly important, for they are more specifically needed in a cultural climate such as ours.

A sermon is always in a sense autobiographical, for in it the preacher bares his own mind and soul so that in the process others may think and feel along with him. It is an invitation to "Come, explore along with me." So any presentation of sermons must be done with humility and yet with hope. This is the nature of the preacher's task, and in that light these sermons are presented for examination as an indication of what one has done and as a clue to what others may do.

THE ETERNAL PRELUDE

"ONE WHO COMES AFTER ME." *John 1:24*

Each year we come to Easter morning with a sense of unexplainable hope. We sense new life in the world of nature. New life flows through the budding trees. We glory in the fragrance of the fresh buds and new beauty of the flowers that decorate our church. We scratch around in our gardens and feel personal achievement when the first row of radishes breaks through the ground. Yet we are too wise to think that our inexplicable hope is tied up with trees, flowers, or vegetables. Surely, they are but symbols of it. They are the visible counterparts of an "invincible surmise" of our innermost soul—that life is drawn toward some rich and meaningful future, rather than anchored to some deadening past.

We cannot explain the power of the life of John the Baptist, apart from his sense of the future. He came alone out of the desert, with a vision in his eye and sharp words upon his tongue. Few of his words are left, but every one of them called men from the death of the past to the life of the future. Like a meteor across the scroll of history,

135

his life and words burned with one message. Like a man possessed by a haunting spirit, he spoke fearlessly of the present with his eyes toward the future. His life was committed to the future. The direction of his living was revealed in those simple words, "There comes one after me."

John here shows us the essential ingredient of immortality. He lived in the future and accepted responsibility for it. He sought consciously to shape it, to make it good. His brief ministry was an earnest plea for others to share his sense of the future and to make themselves ready for its greater revelation.

We have just come through a week filled with the illustrations of frustration and defeat that grow from that strange inability of men to move from the past into the future. Judas could not forget those hopes of the past that saw him raised to political power, so he betrayed his Master and destroyed himself. Joseph could not separate himself from the traditions of his class, and instead of moral victory the best he could do was to furnish a tomb. Pilate could not free himself from the traditions of political expediency and sold both his soul and Roman law cheaply. Peter shook with fear of those who condemned his past associations and looked forward to nothing better than a return to his boat and his fishing nets.

The sense of the future that was so much a part of Pentecost did not come until the disciples learned to cut themselves off from the past and live in terms of the future. Pentecost came when the disciples were able to say, "There comes one after me," rather than, "I do not know the man."

The change in the lives and attitudes of the disciples was the result of a new attitude toward the future. No longer were they like Lot's wife—continually uncertain, embittered,

and off balance, because the⋯ ⋯ ⋯ at life over
their shoulders as they ran awa⋯ ⋯ 'onger were
they whipped by the present, bec⋯ ⋯ not see
beyond it. They looked toward a f⋯ ⋯ possibility and could say, "And in the las⋯ ⋯ be."
Those last days were ahead, not behind. ⋯ 'ife
was changed. Their minds were turned abou⋯ ⋯
the impulse of John the Baptist, and the mi⋯

Any adequate sense of the future involves obli⋯
cannot be aware of the future's possibilities and i⋯
demands. In a very real way, our eternal life begins⋯
we gear our living to the future. Our immortality ⋯
spiritual achievement is a response to the goal of a City ⋯
God, rather than a fright-full life that turns in despair
toward the City of Destruction.

Sometimes we find this insight in unexpected places.
Evans Carlson, the leader of the Marine Raiders, probably
risked his life for his men more often than any other field
grade officer in the services. His awareness of the danger of
fear of the future was summed up in these words to his pastor father: "Those who cringe from death deserve to die, for
they lack the faith and the breadth of vision to be useful
in life." These are ruthless words, but they point out how
inseparably heroism is bound to the future and cowardice
to the past. Some months before he gave his life, in seeking
to rescue from the ocean a person he had never seen before,
the poet Robert Welch penned these significant lines:

With steps that would be constant, we strive as on we fare,
To make our toiling worship, to make our resting prayer.
Reluctant at hard places, to wince with tightened lips;
Who knows what rocky Patmos holds our Apocalypse.

The heroic impulse in life is a response to obligation that can only be met by a faith in the future. Nothing is worth living for or dying for if the human spirit is not moving toward some future realization that makes our best a sane and reasonable response to living. The man whose only loyalty is to the habits and appetites that have chained his whole being to the past knows no inspiration, feels no elation, sees no visions, and lives half buried in his fears of death. Truly death for him means the ending of the past rather than the beginning of the future.

How easily our minds take refuge in the past. It takes no imagination and little courage to defend the past, because so vast a majority are bridled to it. How much easier and more popular to revert to the waste of war rather than to explore for peace. How much easier and how much more profitable to exploit our resources for the falsehoods of the present than to sacrifice for the goals of the future. How much easier to submit to the demands of a life-destroying habit that binds us to the past than to live with a free mind and heart in hope of the better days that better habits can bring.

St. Paul knew the demands Jesus put upon life. He recognized the larger discipline of the future. He said that short-sighted men of affairs "killed the pioneer of life." It was the heroic action of exploring the possibilities of living in a more abundant future, rather than the constricting ideas of the past, that brought Jesus into the hands of the guardians of the past. They were the ones who looked to the darkness of the past and loved that darkness better than the light. They were the ones who turned their backs on the possibility of the realized Messiah, because it meant the wrenching of their thinking from the past they knew to the future they were afraid to know.

An adequate approach to the future is an act of faith. The future is where men adventure to test the truth they know. Nothing great is done without faith in the future. Tradition-bound scientists had solemnly approved the statement that heavier-than-air craft could not fly, but two young men with a sense of the future took off from the sands at Kitty Hawk. Men dedicated to the methods of the past killed each other in the Franco-Prussian War; a young man with faith in the future risked his life to develop a serum to prevent rabies. While men whose minds were rooted in the past said pain was an essential discipline of life, a young dentist with eyes toward the future had the courage to endure persecution that future generations might know the blessings of anesthesia. It takes faith to explore the frontiers of the future in human experience. But when we do, we begin to live immortal lives even here and now.

As Jesus looked at his followers, he pitied their lack of faith. "O ye of little faith," he said. When faith is realized, the future becomes the kingdom of challenging life. John knew it: "There cometh one after me." Jesus knew it: "I go to prepare a place for you."

Parenthood often gives long glimpses of the unexplored future. He who shares the life of youth stays young. The spirit of youth keeps the past from becoming too important and makes the future perpetually interesting. Parental sacrifice helps to keep one foot inside the door of the future. Many parents understand the spirit of the poet's question to the old bridge builder:

> "You have crossed the chasm deep and wide.
> Why build you a bridge at eventide?"
> And the builder raised his old gray head:
> "Good friend, on the path I have come," he said,
> "There followeth after me today

A youth whose feet will pass this way.
This stream, which has been as naught to me,
To that fair-haired boy may a pitfall be;
He, too, must cross in the twilight dim—
Good friend, I am building this bridge for him."

Redemption is bound to the future and gains its value there. "I have come that ye might have life." "Forgetting those things that are past, let us press on." We are redeemed that our lives may produce fruit worthy of redemption in the only place that they can produce—the future. Redemption is a process, and a process is always drawing the future into the present. We work, we produce, we achieve as we face toward our destiny as spiritual beings.

So Easter morning comes to us with no sense of mockery. The symbolism of spring is a counterpart of that newness of life we seek within ourselves. We seek a redemption that sloughs off the debris of a fettering past and fills us with a new sense of the life we may have. Easter reveals again the truth we should never forget—that we are drawn by an ennobling future rather than chained to the past.

Each of us is aware of the unfulfilled nature of our own living. We may not be sure why we are uncertain, unhappy, and unredeemed. We may not be quite sure where the fault lies, but we do not escape the haunting knowledge that life is not all it could be.

For many of us our own personalities have tremendous unrealized possibilities. We carry about the weight of grudges, resentments, and unforgiven sins. We face each new day with fears about ourselves, our health, our habits, and our way of living. We make the future forlorn and uninviting by the bitterness and rejection we crowd into it from the past we do not escape.

Easter comes to your personal living with a new sense of hope, for it can tell you how to make the future a radiant possibility. New health comes into the life that seeks God's will so completely that all else becomes secondary. When God's love works in and through you, the past makes no destructive claims upon you. Certainly, you have a past, but you use it rather than having it abuse you. Your past is transformed from a problem of life to part of its solution when your point of reference in personal living is God. Then your life grows toward its unrealized possibilities, because it is drawn on by God's will and is not held back by your own sense of fear or unworthiness. Easter, for you, may mean the realization of new life for the rest of your life.

Easter may mean a new life in your home. So often our homes are cruelly marred by persistent reference to the past. Some unfortunate deed, some mistake, some circumstance that is a part of life long since gone, may continue to cast its shadow over every thought and act of the home's life. Some past bitterness may keep the full measure of love from expressing itself in the joy of living together for the best future. This Easter may mean for you a turning of your back upon that cruel and crippling fact of the past, because you have learned that the only life that can become abundant for you lies in a future that is freed by God from the destruction of any past. You may today learn how to think of husband or wife or child in a new light, to see them clearly as it were for the first time, because you are seeing them in terms of their life to be rather than their life that was. Yes, Easter may mean a new home for you.

Easter may mean new health for you. Too often persons make themselves ill because they would rather be ill than accept the responsibility of the future. There are those persons, nervously ill, who seek to escape the future by devising an illness, having discovered somewhere in the past that illness relieves them of their duties. Many of the persons Jesus healed were possessed of such devils of enslavement to a life-destroying past. He freed them of the unhealthy love of sympathy and the desire to escape responsibility by making them stand up and face the future. This Easter may be the open door for you to move beyond your cherished ill health to an honest facing of your own rich destiny in courageous and effective living.

Easter may mean for you a new idea of community living. At work, at school, in your business dealings, you may have been deluded by some of the false aims and low judgments inherited from the past. You may think that money is an end in itself, or that power over people is the right of the ruthless. You may have been bequeathed the fallacy that violence is a fit method for making people do your will. Today you may gain the insight and wisdom that leads you to see beyond that heritage to new ideals of living with people. You may grow to see others as children of God, valuable in themselves, and workers together with you in building God's kingdom. No longer, then, will you be able to take a shabby refuge in prejudices or in those mis-representations and misunderstandings that the past would give you as equipment for judging matters of race, creed, or color. You will have learned that maturity of spirit which measures men not in terms of their origins but in terms of their goals.

Yes, Easter appeals to the restless soul within us that is not satisfied with the life we have been living and wants to grow toward something better. It invites us to cast off the chains of the past, unleash the resources of the present, and move out into the depth of life as a God-centered, God-motivated individual.

Life need not be a matter of past tragedies. The indwelling of the Holy Spirit acts as a neutralizing agent for the past. As bad as it may have been, it cannot prevent the grace of God from working in you to make the future better. Before the Archives Building in Washington there is a statue of a woman turning the last pages of a book. Under the statue are the words, "All that is past is prelude, the future begins now." We may feel that we are near the last pages of life's book, but new possibilities and great privileges for life are our unrealized endowment. Do not let this Easter pass without opening the doors to your unused spiritual possibilities.

Our troubled world needs the message of Easter. Our future as a nation and as a family of nations is cramped into the mold of outworn thinking. We cannot face the possibilities of a world of peace and good will, because we keep looking over our shoulders toward national sovereignties, military alliances, and the fear of loss of prestige. But the future comes to those who are ready for it. Let us turn our eyes toward God's untried plans for brotherhood, where men are valued as men and love supplants fear as the basis for action. Peace is tied to God's future rather than to the past fears of men. Plenty for all is found in God's ideal of justice and equality rather than in the exploitations so characteristic of the past. The hope of a workable United Nations Organization is rooted in a discipline of understanding, rather than in our inherited mood of suspicion, fear, and distrust.

Jesus revealed the tremendous power of a life dominated

by a faith in God's ability to sustain the soul that trusts completely in him. He lived that faith. He died that faith, and because of that faith he could not be kept dead. He lived a life that could not end, for the past had no part of it, and death is always a thing of the past. Jesus lived beyond the man-made measurements of time and space. He lived in a world of spiritual values, sharing the nature of God, his Father. We, too, may live our lives with a primary concern for spiritual values. The way is open for us. We make the choice.

Eternal life is no great mystery. It is the faith in life that refuses to be tied to the past. It is the life that rejects the limitations of the past and accepts the possibilities of the future. That life is possible for you. It is possible for you beginning now. Eternal life is a rejection of the mechanical devices for measuring life in favor of the spiritual values that measure eternity.

Here is the meaning of Easter for you. It is life free of a deadening past. It is life that is eternal because even now it shares eternal values. It is life lived in conscious companionship with God, for the purposes God reveals. Thus it is life with an unshaken sense of purpose that keeps it moving into the future with confidence and faith, freed from any power of the past to darken or destroy. In fact, it is immortal life for you, beginning now and enduring "from henceforth even for evermore."

THE CHOICE IS OURS

"YOU WILL KNOW THE TRUTH, AND THE TRUTH WILL MAKE YOU FREE." *John 8:32*

Those who make a special study of insects point out that in nearly every respect the insect is superior to man. For its size the insect is much stronger than a man. In its ability to accomplish useful ends, the insect is more intelligent than man. When it comes to ordering its social life, many insects have a model-community existence. It may well be that unless we quickly learn to control our destructive powers, the capacity for survival among the insects may cause them to inherit the earth. The artistry of the spider, the industry of the bee, and the ordered existence of the ant are not the minor wonders of nature. Yet, with all their abilities, there is one thing insects lack—the ability to remember or the capacity of forethought. They exist as automata of instinct.

The capacity for ordered thought and free choice seems to be an endowment of man alone. Yet the one place where we are superior is the one place where we run into most difficulty. Have you ever felt any concern about your freedom of choice? Have you ever been bothered by a feeling

145

that some power beyond your conscious control was at work within you to determine your action? Have you ever done something and then tried to examine the forces that led you to do as you did?

Men have long struggled with this problem of freedom of choice. The ancient philosophers felt that all philosophical understanding was dependent upon the power of the mind to exert its influence freely. Modern psychology, through its study of personality, has thrown light on the nature of the conscious and unconscious forces that tend to influence behavior.

Wherever men's minds have come to grips with the basic problems of life, they have had to face this problem of freedom of choice. The fatalist and the predestinarian on one side try to resolve the dilemma by the belief that their life is predetermined by a cosmic force so great and all encompassing that they are completely subject to it and never able to move beyond its inexorable control. The thinker who approaches life in terms of ethical values feels that they are empty and meaningless unless man is capable of the type of choices that are a part of moral living. So also, the philosopher of religion feels that the sensitive nature of man's questing soul is a cosmic joke unless that sensitivity can be expressed in an exercise of freedom.

These two approaches to the subject have been expressed in that sharp and economical expression that is the poet's forte. Don Marquis presents the view of the philosophical determinist in these words:

> I say that I choose for myself,
> But that is an idle boast,
> For here in my house of being
> Ghost is at war with ghost.

Old loves and hates at the core of me,
Old doubts and faiths in the brain,
And salt in the stinging blood of me
Old lusts revive again.
I say that I am myself,
But what is this self of mine
But a knot in the tangled skein of things
That chance and chance combine?

John Oxenham presents the ethical and religious judgment concerning the soul of man as a residence for freedom in his lines,

To every man there openeth
A Way, and Ways, and a Way.
The High Soul climbs the High Way
The Low Soul gropes the Low,
And in between, on the misty flats,
The rest drift to and fro.
But to every man there openeth
A High Way and a Low,
And every man decideth
The Way his soul shall go.

As is always the case with extremes, the truth probably lies somewhere in between. And even those who argue most vigorously for determinism seem to like to act as if they were free to make important choices.

One does not live long without being aware of the limits placed on his freedom of choice. Many of the most important factors of life are completely beyond our control. We do not choose our parents, our sex, or our native land. We must accept much of our educational system and our religious heritage. These are all, of course, major determinants of any role we play in life. We must, then, admit that many elements in life are clearly determined by forces beyond our control.

On the other hand, we sense that the whole course of life may be changed by seemingly trivial circumstances. It is recorded that Sam Houston was snubbed by a red-headed beauty at a dance in Tennessee. He stormed out of the dance hall and did not stop until he got to Texas and even then had enough emotion left to lead a revolution. A trivial circumstance can loom large in personal life and national history. A slight accident or even a hunch may change the course of a life. It is rather irrational to believe that any predetermining cosmic force would be dependent upon such trivia to chart our course through life.

Man's quest for emotional and intellectual security seems to drive him toward rigid formulas for explaining the phenomena of existence. From limited information he develops a theory that may not be warranted but may satisfy a personal need. This tendency is found not only among philosophers and psychologists, but often among those who claim to be purely scientific but do not quite escape a desire to be philosophers of science. Men are not long satisfied with the theories they build. The definition of life is always more than its description. The needs of the total man are always greater than the limitations a rigid system will bear. In his very dissatisfaction with the theories he builds and then destroys, the mind of man gives a courageous testimony to its belief in a measure of freedom.

A renowned astronomer, after looking at the order of the stars in their courses, looks at man and says,

Absolute metaphysical freedom would make human action altogether unpredictable. What we ordinarily mean by the

> freedom of the will appears to be very much better de-
> scribed by a current political tag, "self-determination." We
> hold a man responsible, and therefore "free." . . . If our
> personal freedom and responsibility are illusions, so is the
> blue sky above us and the solid earth beneath our feet.
> Let the keen analyst pursue his unending search for the
> elusive ultimate; we rest upon the proximate. Our freedom
> is, at the least, as sure as sunrise, as solid as rock, as im-
> movable as the eternal hills; need we ask more? *

The religious mind seeks to approach both the facts of
nature and the needs of man with a concern for the total
life of man. To see life and see it whole, he seeks to build
on a firm middle ground between rigid determinism and an
absolute and uncontrolled freedom. He well knows that he
is not perfectly free, and is not frightened by the prospect.
He also knows that he is not absolutely determined and is
not apprehensive of the responsibility implied. His very self-
consciousness makes him responsive, and if responsive then
charged with responsibility, and responsibility predicates a
measure of freedom.

It is within this rather limited and clearly defined area of
freedom that we would focus our thinking. Within this area
the choices are made that can be made. Here, between un-
limited freedom and complete determinism, we are obliged
to live our lives as responsible individuals and responsible
members of the group. Here we cannot excuse ourselves
from blame or delegate those responsibilities that are pe-
culiarly our own. Here our limited freedom leads to un-
limited consequences. The mariner does not have to have
every foot of his ship under his direct control so long as he
controls the rudder. His mastery is determined by his skill

* H. N. Russell, *Fate and Freedom* (Yale University Press, 1927), pp.
49, 50, 57.

in handling the rudder so that the bulk of the ship goes where he wants it to go in spite of winds or currents.

Our ability to use this capacity for free choice within limited bounds becomes the measure of our capacity to function effectively. The finer the degree of control, the more effectively may we function. A baseball pitcher has limited freedom. He must pitch the ball within the pre-scribed area indicated by the width of the plate and the height of the batter. But the great pitcher is the one who can use his limited area of freedom with a control that shaves the corners and with a change of pace that baffles the batter. His mastery within limited areas of control available to him determines whether or not he is able to win games.

The scientist works with a large amount of given data and major areas of the unpredictable. He cannot tell where a single atom will be a split second hence. But within the area of his knowledge, he disciplines himself so as not to violate the infinite number of laws of nature that prescribe his work. Rather, he seeks to use his understanding and imagination so wisely, in the clearly defined areas within which he must work, that he may cooperate successfully with the basic laws he is seeking to fulfill.

The social philosopher in theory and the politician in practice work within the clearly defined boundaries of an inherited social structure. They are not free to make un-limited changes because of the resistance to change that seems to be a part of man's inheritance. But he is able to work within the bounds of the social structure to protect its long-range values at the very same time he is working to improve immediate conditions. He is free only insofar as he acts wisely, with understanding and foresight.

The religious soul, like the scientist and philosopher, works within the bounds of the given. His own needs and his awareness of them, his sensitivity to the needs and rights of others, and his awareness of a cosmic factor that defines his threefold relationship to self, others, and the Universe can never be ignored. It is the platform on which he stands when he exercises the freedom that is a part of his God-consciousness.

The responsibility for choice is a heavy burden on man. History has shown that again and again he has tried to escape the burden of his freedom. He has sold his birthright for a mess of pottage to those who promised him some form of security in return for his freedom. The history of recent decades shows millions of the earth's people exchanging their freedom for the assurances of a demagogue. The very basis for democracy is threatened by a disposition to flee from its burdensome privileges.

The history of the Christian Church has revealed the devices of men used to escape the burden of responsibility for choice. Every generation seems to have produced its own brand of "theological marihuana," to make plausible its escape from the burdens of freedom by retreat into a world of intellectual pipe dreams and pious sophistry. Whether it be ecclesiastical authoritarianism or a theology of determinism, the result is similar.

Yet this privilege and this burden are so innately a part of the nature of man that he cannot effectively deny it. His denials deny him, and whether it be in scientific theory or religious practice, he inevitably comes to the place where his life needs make ineffective his efforts to deny his freedom. The highway of the future is open to those men and that people who accept the full burden of freedom. When the genius and the energy that has been invested in denial or compromise are used to give direction to the freedom he possesses, man will stand in awe before the nature of his privilege and will the more seek the guidance that comes from clear and complete devotion to the source of his privilege. Perhaps this represents the basic problem of our time, and the myriad minor problems that are spawned by it will not be dealt with adequately until man accepts the burden of his freedom under God.

As we look at this highway into the future, with its burdens of both privilege and responsibility, we ask first, "What are the ingredients of the fine choices that can best utilize our measure of freedom?" We respond at once that these choices must be the product of the total positive response of man to life. When man's approach is purely intellectual, he may use his mind to deny his spirit. When it is purely emotional, he may ignore the essential restraints that are a part of mental discipline. Fine choices, if they are to be the essence of the good life, must combine the best judgments of the mind with those creative emotions that stem from the spirit of man. The quality of this emotional response may well change the impact of the mind upon the experience of life. It is not only important to have the right facts. It is also necessary to feel the right feelings. These right feelings do not spring full-blown from the soul of man but are the product of that positive faith and clear understanding that are united in the religious spirit. As with the other great basic concepts of life like space and time, this quality of spirit is difficult to define and easy to see in action.

When this quality of spirit is added to education, the nature and quality of the educational process changes. When the Little Professor of Piney Woods started his school for Negro children in Mississippi, he had not only the equipment of his own education, he had what was more important: a great faith and a deep love. On his first day Dr. Jones sat on one end of a log with a small boy on the other end, and learning was dispensed with love. The years fulfilled that relationship in a school that has brought forth the best in many youths and has given the world more than its share of qualified leaders. Those who have studied the work at Piney Woods and have been impressed with its achievements, have found the important ingredient to be not an unusual mastery of the technical aspects of educational procedure, but rather the inspiring quality of the love and understanding with which each pupil was met. The success was dependent more upon the quality of the God-determined spirit than upon the self-determined mind.

No one would doubt the significance of the scientific contribution of Dr. Albert Schweitzer to the study and treatment of tropical disease. But when one thinks of him, it is not primarily as a scientist, for the significance of his life lies in the application of scientific knowledge with love. His reverence for life is hard to conceive of as an intellectually determined attitude alone. It breathed so much of the quality of disciplined emotions that it moved his life beyond the realm of artful science to a high plane of the greater art of living in response to a divine plan. His goals were calculated more because of his world view than because of himself.

Few would deny the great contribution of Fritz Kreisler to the world of music. But among music lovers he holds a special place, for he is a symbol of fine music expressed with love. He auctioned his fine library of manuscripts and violins, including his Stradivarius, that the proceeds might be used by a hospital. His simple life and his use of only a small portion of his income for personal needs has been a revelation of that disciplined feeling. The quality of his life was more than a response to the discipline of his art. He was responsive to a higher art, that of living by a choice of large spiritual goals.

To explain the responses of great men of science, education, or the arts as a matter of determinism is difficult. The small mathematics of determinism does not fit the grandeur of such human souls. To define the substance of fine choices as merely intellectual leaves much unexplained. The fine choices that mark the fine life are the fruit of the personality that loves God with heart and soul and mind and strength, and neighbor as one's self. These fine choices always represent a plus factor in life. Here are the three levels of sum-total responsiveness and acceptance. Effective self-determination cannot be achieved without effective self-acceptance. Creative social relations are not achieved apart from a healthy capacity to relate one's self to those other persons who are a part of one's life. A fruitful spiritual life is not reasonable apart from that acceptance of the universe that is expressed through an inspiring Creator-creature relationship.

An insight into the psychological factors that guide men's minds might lead us to believe that those who are afraid of freedom and its responsibilities, consciously or unconsciously use philosophy as a defense mechanism, and retreat to the security of determinism, fatalism, mechanism, or behaviorism. It may not be expressed in such terms, for some would put their philosophy of life into a simple question, "What difference does it make?" Inversely, those who have learned the art of accepting life positively and live with a large measure of love, are not afraid of the burden of choice. They welcome the privilege of freedom, because they feel that they can be instruments in God's hands for fulfilling his claims upon life.

The fine choices of life, then, would be a product of the mind that possesses the truth that makes minds free. It would involve also that integrity of mind and emotion that moves ahead into life without fear. It would employ a capacity for spiritual sensitivity that would respond to the souls of others and the soul of the universe. For this compassion brings to its finest fruitage the efforts of educator, scientist, artist, and the religious personality.

Viewed from the point of ethical judgment, then, the problem becomes not so much whether or not we have the freedom to make choices, but whether or not we have the courage to use the freedom we have wisely. When a young Galilean prayed, "Father, not my will, but thine, be done," he was expressing the greatest of freedoms of the human will, that of relating itself to a greater will, a cosmic entity, the personality of God.

A century ago, when a great crisis was upon us as a nation, a man with a courage that did not seek escape in ambiguities or philosophical denial wrote a poem, "The Present Crisis." Some lines from it indicate the mood and the burden of the free soul as he faces the awe-full task of using his freedom.

New occasions teach new duties; Time makes ancient good
    uncouth;
They must upward still, and onward, who would keep abreast
    of Truth. . . .
Once to every man and nation comes the moment to decide,

In the strife of Truth with Falsehood, for the good or evil
   side. . . .
Truth forever on the scaffold, Wrong forever on the throne,
Yet that scaffold sways the future, and, behind the dim unknown,
Standeth God within the shadow, keeping watch above his
   own. . . .
They enslave their children's children who make compromise
   with sin.

Our day brings its thrilling challenges. Decisions that
will be important for future generations must be made. The
future belongs to those persons who approach it with clear
thinking, integrity, and spiritual sensitivity. The ambiguous
and the unsure are the same as those who deny their
freedom. They are unworthy of it. But uncertainty and
denial are never adequate escapes from real responsibility.

We are not insects. We are endowed with reason and a
capacity for choice. We have the burden of using our
freedom and responsibility to make the finest choices.
Ultimately there is no escape from freedom. There is only
the claim upon us to realize and fulfill our nature as self-
conscious, social-conscious, and God-conscious souls. We
cannot deny our very nature. We must fulfill it.

The choice is ours.

THE VIA DOLOROSA—A WAY OF MASTERY OVER SUFFERING

"DO NOT WEEP FOR ME, BUT WEEP FOR YOURSELVES."
Luke 23:28

Sooner or later every one of us must come to grips with the problem of suffering. So much suffering seems to be a part of human experience that we must develop the resources for mastering it, or it may master us. We may readily accept the cause-effect relation that follows sinful action, but it is more difficult for us to deal with the evident injustice and tragic consequences of the suffering of the innocent which seems to have no valid reason.

Mankind has long struggled with this problem and has come up with a variety of answers. The philosopher tries to rationalize suffering, and the hedonist tries to escape it. The cynic sneers at both life and its suffering, while the religious person faces suffering and tries to use it creatively even if he cannot explain it.

It was a philosopher who said, "To those who think, life is comedy; to those who feel, life is tragedy." Buddha

157

indicated that existence and suffering are one and the same thing. The writer of the Book of Job says,

> For affliction does not come from the dust,
>   nor does trouble sprout from the ground;
> but man is born to trouble
>   as the sparks fly upward.

When Jesus moved from his trial to his execution, those who lined the Via Dolorosa wept and he rebuked them, saying, "Do not weep for me, but weep for yourselves." He had clear enough understanding of his suffering to know it was not clearly as tragic as the abject suffering of those who suffered with no purpose. His purpose was clear, so the cross was not tragedy but triumph. Those who wept saw nothing but the tragedy and were overcome by it. That was tragedy indeed.

Jesus lived in a world where suffering was rampant. There was unbridled sadism and cruelty. Authority was administered with brutality, and fear was considered an adequate tool of control. Government was insensitive to the needs of individuals and because there was no semblance of democratic control, there was widespread irresponsibility with resultant suffering, injustice, and poverty.

It was a world where anesthesia was unknown and physical suffering had to be accepted in the raw for there was no other way. Inadequate understanding led men to false concepts of illness as a form of punishment, and the diseases of the emotions were treated as if they were criminal behavior. Steeped in ignorance, fear, and superstition, they had difficulty in developing a structure of right relations between cause and effect, illness and suffering, tragedy and triumph. Tradition equated illness with divine disfavor and providence with divine blessing. It was not until Jesus uttered his skeptical judgments on the values of the past that there was any revision of this thinking.

At three definite points Jesus rejected the judgments of the past in relation to suffering. When questioned by his followers, "Who sinned, this man or his parents, that he was born blind?" Jesus answered, "It was not that this man sinned, or his parents, but that the works of God might be made manifest in him. We must work the works of him who sent me." Sin is ruled out as the only cause of calamity. The healing, fulfilling, creative power is the power of health and proper function and right relations. Speaking of man's innocent involvement in cause-effect relationships, he answers the disciples, who thought Pilate had punished the more wicked, by saying, "Do you think that these Galileans were worse sinners than all the other Galileans . . . ? I tell you, No. . . . Or those eighteen upon whom the tower in Siloam fell . . . were worse offenders than all the others who dwelt in Jerusalem? I tell you, No." Here in the first few verses of the thirteenth chapter of Luke he points out that the calamities that come from man and nature do not prove that people who suffer are sinful. This was a revolutionary idea. It was contrary to the thinking of the day, yet it has become the basis for the whole structure of the healing arts. Therapy, sympathy, kindness, and a helpful attitude toward the misfortunes that are so much a part of the life of mankind are dependent upon the acceptance of this new and far-reaching idea of Jesus.

It is difficult for us to grasp the implications of such a revolutionary doctrine in our world with its highly developed medical practice and its care for the sick and suffering. Try to imagine the attitude that would reject all of this as a violation of the will of God, an interference with the divine plan of the universe. A physician would be chief of sinners, the compassionate would be suspect, and the sufferer would merely be getting his just deserts.

Let us be clear at this point. There is no effort in the words of Jesus to deny the nature of a cause-effect relationship at work in the universe. Much of his suffering man brings upon himself by not doing the good he knows. But if he were able to live up to the full measure of his understanding of righteousness, there would be much suffering left that is not determined by his being good or bad, wise or foolish, worthy or unworthy. There are important natural factors to which man must adjust. "The rain falls on the just and on the unjust." In the twenty-first chapter of Luke these factors at work in life to cause suffering without regard to guilt or innocence are outlined.

Many suffer as a result of false religious teaching. The innocent bear much of the burden of war and conflict in human society. Hurricanes, earthquakes, and other physical calamities strike without regard for the convenience of man or the situation of the innocent. Physical illness and the infirmities of age are visited on men without consideration of quality of character. Economic distress brings suffering to good and bad alike. Man's inhumanity to man starts chain reactions that reach far beyond those who are at first involved. The misuse of power by irresponsible authority places staggering burdens on the innocent. The trials of home life bring heartache and suffering to many. Those who accept the insights of high religion often suffer persecution because of their devotion to principle. We do not have time to elaborate on these forces at work in life, but you sense the reach and burden of such suffering by merely mentioning it. Suffice it to say that with the clear recognition of these forces at work in life with no regard for what we consider moral selection, we have made a clear step forward in the human struggle against suffering. A clear distinction is often the important first step toward understanding.

Men have had difficulty keeping these revolutionary ideas clearly in their minds through the centuries. The Puritans reverted to a similar type of thinking in their belief that virtue was rewarded with prosperity while evil was revealed through poverty. Within the last century efforts have been made to prevent the use of anesthetics, because it would deny man the chastening benefits of suffering. Even now there are those who would, through the use of outworn religious concepts, prevent the easing of mental suffering. But by and large men have come to accept the idea that there is a large amount of suffering that is not related to any moral problem. It is due to man's finiteness, the limits of his understanding of the universe, and the quality of his creaturehood. He may seek to relieve and limit this suffering, but he is under no sense of guilt for it himself, nor has he a right to pass an unfavorable judgment on others because of it.

How, then, does this bring us to face the matter of suffering in our own paradoxical age? Our age is the most brutal in human history. We have witnessed more unnecessary destruction of human life and more unreasonable suffering inflicted on innocent persons in the past two generations than ever before in human history. Perhaps our feelings are not so depraved, but our equipment for implementing our feelings is greater than ever before. By a show of hands in a legislative hall we can determine whether or not millions of innocent persons will suffer hunger. At the urging of an unbalanced demagogue the lives of millions are destroyed. We do not like to pass such a judgment on the day in which we live, but we cannot change the arithmetic nor deny the facts of recent history.

Yet this is also the age that has given expression to more humanitarian effort than any other. This is an era of widespread philanthropy, compassion, and concern. We have invested our time and energy and our means in an unrelenting struggle against the physical forms of suffering. We have advanced the healing arts to relieve the sufferers. We have organized societies to express a special concern for nearly every part of the human anatomy. Our strange power of group destructiveness on the one hand is balanced by a deep concern and passionate desire to help the sufferer on the other. That fact alone can give a clue to the uncertainty and confusion that exist, for by this bifurcation at the level of action we have done irreparable damage to our feeling capacity. We limit the areas of acute physical suffering through medical science at the same time that we extend physical suffering through military science. Is it any wonder that we have increased the areas of psychological and spiritual suffering to an all-time high? Is it any wonder that our age will probably come to be known as the era of the great heartache?

How do we face this matter of the great paradox of our age? How do we react to the emotional confusion caused by the compulsive control of life by a destructive force so great that we cannot seem to master it? Do we feel guilty about it and so add to our other burdens an unbearable sense of guilt? Or do we try to move beyond the dilemma through creative action? It would be an evidence of a group neurosis to assume a guilt for which there is no clear responsibility. The sane and healthy attitude would be to move ahead to a large enough world view to give us a point of focus well beyond the confusion created by our dilemma.

Our great tragedy is that we have too small a religion, too small an ideal to which to devote ourselves. We have not even grown to the place where we will accept the universality taught by Jesus that would remove all of the artificial barriers men build between themselves. These artificial boundaries create infinite suffering. We have not been willing to admit the religious errors that merely fortify our injurious judgments. We have hoped for some kind of miracle to resolve our problems, when we have the resources within ourselves but failed to use them. Rather than move back toward a crippling guilt we need to move ahead to a releasing faith.

The adequacy of a world view gives men a larger and more adequate purpose for living. The women who wept by the Via Dolorosa wept superficial tears for a small purpose. They saw a man suffering and their emotions were touched. Jesus saw their small purpose and the small faith behind it and was aware of the deeper tragedy. He suffered with a purpose and his suffering found a meaningful context. They suffered for no great purpose, so their suffering was sheer, undiluted agony with no fact in human experience to relieve it.

The human mind has the resources to project a faith adequate to sustain it no matter what the nature of suffering may be, but these resources are not found in philosophy. Philosophy seeks reasons and an ordered plan for man's existence. Much suffering is unreasoned and unreasonable, clear injustice and beyond man's responsibility. Unless he has more than philosophy can offer, he cannot handle it. Science seeks control, but the very act of extending control in some directions limits it in others. Even the scientist needs something far more satisfying than his science. Jesus gave religious insight. He did not try to explain suffering, much less explain it away. He recognized it, faced it squarely, and urged men to have a large enough view of life to fit the suffering into its proper place and use it creatively. He was reasonable as far as reason went. Then he urged a world view adequate to sustain the best pragmatic efforts of men.

We can illustrate several levels of approach to this matter of suffering. The Buddhists and Christian Scientists, with an inadequate world view, try to fit all suffering into a false category and call it error. They would deny the validity of any such experience of creative suffering as the cross. With a small world view focused about their own small problems, they would try to bend reality to fit their own small needs and their distorted reality concept.

The Stoic goes one step farther. With "head bloody but unbowed," he grits his teeth and affirms his faith in man's ability to suffer with courage and die with dignity. But there is no purpose in it except to show his inner power over external circumstance.

The creative soul takes his suffering and makes of it a thing of beauty. The growing power, insight, and beauty of the symphonies of Beethoven cannot be understood apart from his ability to use the brutal facts of life for creative purposes. He took what life brought, refined it through his creative genius, and gave back to the world something infinitely greater. We are all richer because of what he did with his suffering.

But there is yet another level. With sensitivity and concern, man may move out to accept suffering for a purpose defined by a great world view. We all know of the testimony of a life like Schweitzer's. Probably none of you has heard of the significant life of a young English physician named John Melle. Brilliant in mind, trained with care, skillful in his profession, he was moved by a courageous and selfless spirit. When Mussolini made his brutal attack on the defenseless people of Ethiopia, John Melle was stirred by the injustice of it. He knew of the inadequate medical corps with the Ethiopian army. Without thought for his own welfare he gave up his career in this country, organized a Red Cross unit, and moved into the battle area to bring relief from suffering. Through terrible months he served and retreated with the troops toward Addis Ababa. Although he survived the heat of battle, he was shot in the back by a crazed native who mistakenly assumed that all white men were like Mussolini. John Melle did not want suffering for himself or for anyone else. He lived his life to relieve suffering. His sudden death had the elements of tragedy, but more for the people of Ethiopia than for himself. Somehow sympathy does not seem an adequate emotion with which to view a life with such spiritual grandeur. He feared no suffering but went out to accept it because of a world view that sustained his effort. Any weak sympathy we might express toward him would invite the response, "Do not weep for me, but weep for yourselves."

Religion makes no effort to explain away the fact of suffering. It seeks to bring relief where possible, but it also looks at life realistically enough to know that there are large areas of human suffering that remain as an irrevocable part of existence itself. It would not merely urge us to stand firm and take it with courage. It would indicate a world view, a sense of purpose, so great that we would not shun life for fear of suffering, or hesitate to suffer for a purpose, but rather, with a full use of the creative genius of the human spirit, would refine suffering until it should become a thing of beauty, an undying testimony to the power of the human spirit.

The words, "Do not weep for me, but weep for yourselves," carry a deep meaning. They invite a comparison of suffering in the lives of those with superficial purpose with suffering in the lives of those with great purpose. It points out that suffering is opportunity as well as calamity for those who see life in large enough terms to use even tragedy creatively. There is no easy answer to the problem of suffering. Those who seek easy answers can only confound themselves and travel at a level of superficiality and illusion. The deepest understanding of the nature of God is revealed to those who with keen reality sense look life squarely in the eye and use the resources of their own spirits to make it more abundant.

As Don Marquis, the poet, has indicated, the concept of God is built in the souls of men who have the capacity to feel a great need and the courage to face it honestly.

> Out of agonies and love shall God be made.
> He is wrought of cries that meet between the worlds,
> Of seeking cries that have come forth
> From the cruel spheres to find a God and be stilled.
> For he builds himself of the passion of martyrs,
> And he is woven of the ecstasy of great lovers,
> And he is wrought of the anguish of them that have
>   greatly needed him.

When all of the genius of man has been employed to relieve suffering, the problem will remain, for it is basic to
existence itself. It can make or break a man. An adequate
religious faith can become a basis for self-mastery and mastery over the experience of suffering. Such a faith can help
a man to use suffering rather than be abused by it. It can
make it possible for him to suffer and yet not be destroyed.
Yes, it can even lead him to suffer in such a way that his
suffering becomes a symbol of triumph. When that is done,
the cross assumes its proper place as a meaningful religious
symbol.

The cross as a symbol of triumphant faith is dependent
upon an adequate view of man as a spiritual being, with a
soul responsive to its divine counterpart. Man's mastery over
personal suffering is not realized apart from a firm faith
in the eternal nature of his spiritual sensitivity. That faith
makes his being something more than the sum total of the
incidents of life and guarantees his mastery over that which
is truly incidental.

The symbolic nature of the cross is also dependent upon
a view of the universe that leads man to reverence the structure of law and order, the working of cause and effect, even
where he cannot see that law or cause. He believes that "beyond the dim unknown" there is reason, and that what to
his limited mind is injustice and disorder is not the result
of a cosmic failure or a malicious force, but is rather the
evidence of his own limited capacity to know and judge.

The symbolic nature of the cross is also dependent upon
a view of a Creator who cannot be less than that which he
has created. The finest outreach of man's nature is in the
creative, redeeming, sustaining power of love. As God is

love, so man seeks to fulfill in his own being that creative capacity to respond to life even when it does not seem to respond to him. For he lives ultimately not by sight but by faith which is insight.

So the struggle for mastery goes on between the free spirit of man and the often unfriendly circumstances of life itself. The free spirit seeks to be a great spirit. Ultimately the resources for triumph lie within your own soul.

THE BELIEF IN LIFE THAT DOES NOT END

If life is important, we are impelled to consider the relationship of life to death as a physical fact. The certainty of death does not usually employ much of our thought, although its effect, as it gnaws away at our circle of acquaintances, does persistently raise the question, "If a man die, shall he live again?"

In normal times the insurance companies do their best to keep us reminded of the inevitable. In times such as these, when death comes quickly and violently, we are more apt to take time out to think of the implications of what happens when life stops physically.

The average young person thinks more of life than of death. Perhaps it is a healthy sign when the process of living commands so much attention that we have little thought for anything else. But it is as necessary that we prepare our minds to face the possibility of death as it is to give consideration to our estates. The destructiveness of war forces us to look carefully at the question of the meaning of death and the possibility of some form of continuing life.

"We no longer speak glibly of heaven and hell. A wise agnosticism now chastens our speech about the eternal." We know enough about other religions to know that life after death is not always a pleasant prospect, for in India future life is a haunting tragedy. We also know enough about suffering and pain to know that death often comes as a friend, although we speak of its blessings in hushed tones.

At other times we rebel against the evident injustice of untimely or tragic death and willingly say with the poet, "Thou art much too fair to be death's conquest, and make worms thine heir." If we have not already, we may be certain that we will in the future face the problem and the mystery of death and immortality.

As we meet the problem our attitudes will differ, but they will in all probability fall into one of three classes. There are those who fear death. A notorious publisher is an example of one who dreaded the thought of death so violently that, it is said, he would not even permit the word to be uttered in his presence. That was rather flimsy protection against a sure fate.

Then there are those who take a morbid delight in talking and thinking about death. Some individuals like to prepare their own funeral services long in advance. An organizational expression of the same thing is seen in the other-worldly emphasis of the Church of Rome with its many Masses, candles of memory, confessions, and last rites. The whole structure seems aimed at the inevitable fact of death and the mystery and superstition that so often center about the thoughts of immortality.

And last is the attitude of those souls who take death in their stride because they have undergirded life with a healthy creativity. Henry Thoreau, the lover of nature, is probably too perfect an example of this confidence in life, for when a pious friend asked him on his deathbed if he had made his peace with God, he merely responded that they had never quarreled.

If we want the assurance of a Thoreau, we must work to get it. Not that we can find the final key to understanding, but that we may be prepared to face death, unafraid, as men of faith.

The Christian, of all persons, must have such a faith. He must be prepared to face the paganism that is so evident at some so-called Christian burials. He must face the growing unconcern with the whole question of the value of life. And he must stand ready to interpret life to those who feel the full fury of physical destruction with no spiritual anchor to hold them.

The contemporary world has all of the old skepticisms plus a few of its own. There are many arguments against life after death. There are those who ask how a function can live on after its organ is destroyed, "How can the mind remain when the brain is gone?" And others will ask, "Would you crave eternal life for little Mr. X and his nagging wife?" Still others will contend that an idea of heaven is merely an escape for those who seek to compensate present frustrations with future hopes.

More scientific souls will ask how we can find any prospects for immortality in a universe where human life seems to be an accident, especially as we know through astronomic and geologic research that there was a time when there was no life on the earth, and we can be equally sure that we are moving toward another time when life will be destroyed. What will become of cherished spiritual values on a planet that moves from the uninhabited to the uninhabitable? Those who look at life through an increasingly nonspiritual materialism find less and less place for a concept of immortality.

Even those who seek a semblance of an ethical basis for skepticism say, "Is not a hope of continued life a mere extension of selfishness on the part of the individual?" It is clearly seen that such people do not find it easy to separate themselves from a biological approach to life, which sees only the functioning organism.

The politically and socially minded are apt to say, "Society will live on after me, so if I can contribute anything to culture or a better social order that is all the immortality I want." They too show that they look at life in terms of institutions and make man the means rather than the end.

While the modern mind is critical of a concept that seems to have no scientific basis, it is true that great minds of our day are willing to come to the defense of a belief in life after death. Theologians habitually make a strong defense, probably none more eloquent than Sir Henry Jones in presenting the idea that a good God would not create spiritually sensitive individuals and then leave them stranded in a universe, unconcerned.

The first law of thermodynamics, which finds that energy cannot be destroyed, gives us many a suggestion. If common energy cannot be destroyed but only transferred, why should the creative energy of the human spirit alone face destruction? Then, too, who is to prove or even attempt to prove that spiritual energy does not continue? The world gives much evidence of change of state, but little of destruction.

Still others will claim that emotion is as valid as reason and that emotion, the active force of living, is not satisfied to face the collapse of life. Who is there to say that the rich

emotion expressed by Emerson as he stood beside the life-
less form of his child is not as mature an insight as the
caustic criticism of the scientist?

> What is excellent, as God lives, is permanent;
> Hearts are dust; heart's loves remain
> Heart's love will meet thee again.

The most noble insights of men are not given to scientific
measurement.

Although there is much to strengthen our faith in the
fields of theology, science, and human emotion, I do not
look there for my final proof of the permanence of life. For
me the ethical approach to the problem is most helpful, not
because it is necessarily more true, but just because my mind
moves more easily and satisfyingly in that direction. For
me the central question is not whether life is eternal, but
whether we can make our lives worthy of immortality if it
is real.

Life is not breath—mere persistence. As I see it, the
nub of the problem is not a quantitative extension in time,
but a qualitative extension in value. Not how much, but
how good. Too often we think of immortality as living after
death. We must begin to think of it as the act of living itself.
Its quality alone determines whether it is worthy of surviving
that incident we call death.

The best evidence of this is in the lives of moral men. The
morally defeated seek no future; the morally victorious
fear neither present nor future. Men were shocked to hear of
the death of Col. T. E. Lawrence of Arabia in a motorcycle
accident some years ago. Few realized, however, that here
was a tragic example of a life that had lost value through
moral defeat. As a young archaeologist, Lawrence had given

his talent and courage to his government, and it used him to betray his friends. His sensitive ethical character was so injured by this fraud and injustice that he committed spiritual suicide, changed his name, renounced his rank, his royal decorations, and his former life, and became an airplane mechanic. Life lost meaning when his sensitive ethical nature was stunned.

On the other hand, the words of Socrates on trial for his life breathe a rich sense of the qualitative judgment of the morally healthy soul: "No evil can happen to a good man, either in life or after death." He disdained an effort to escape execution, for the mere quantity of life made little appeal to him.

Is it not true, then, that the burden of proof falls upon us? If we think death is an enemy, we must defeat it by making life good, not in terms of a Methuselah but of a Christ.

The fullest satisfaction of the ethical approach comes through the life and leadership of Jesus. He lived a sublime life of confidence in quality. He lived sure that underneath were the everlasting arms. When death met him face to face, he could say, "Father, into thy hands I commit my spirit." We look at this example of courage and confidence and see a clue to that larger meaning of immortality.

Yet, when we hear the promise, "I go to prepare a place for you," we have been too willing to measure it by our crass material idea of a heaven in space and time. Jesus was not a geographer. Deeper is the meaning that we can see only in the qualitative—that life is made secure for us through the example of one who saw the eternal in the reckless living of the life of God within the limitations of man-made measurements of time.

We cannot expect to build for ourselves a satisfying concept of eternal life unless we rid our minds of those habits of
measurement which do not take into account the quality
of living. So often we try to approach the qualitative concepts of the spiritual life with quantitative presuppositions.
We make the problems complicated and harrowing. We
carry on fruitless investigations and expend unnecessary
energy. We crawl on all fours as animals rather than stand
as spiritual entities.

Jesus has pointed with confidence to an interpretation of
life that will hold all our weight—that will meet our needs.
He has shown an interpretation of the eternal which rests
not in time but in value.

If we would face the problem of death in the light of
Christian truth, our preoccupation would be not solely with
rites and sorrows at the end of the physical phase of living.
Rather our thought would be upon the lives we are living
in the here and now. We would try to hew out of the piece
of time allotted us a character that measured life in terms
of its possibilities and its spiritual goal. Then we would
be able to say in honest wonder, "O death, where is thy
sting? O grave, where is thy victory?" Death would be an
incident, and life would have risen to its full stature, confi-
dent in the present purpose as well as the future goal. There
would be no more cringing in fear but rather walking in
faith.

Do you want this life of immortality? This faith? This
sense of quality? Then live in terms of quality, beginning
now. Then dispel fear with faith, now. Then know that you
are in the midst of an eternal venture, now. Then believe
in a human spirit that need not die, now or ever.

THE INDWELLING SPIRIT

"THE WORD WAS MADE FLESH, AND DWELT AMONG US."
John 1:14

This morning I want to think with you about the indwelling of God's Spirit in man. This is not an easy subject to talk about, because it is difficult to move the idea from the abstract to the concrete. Yet it is so important for our living that we must try to make the idea live and move and have its being before our eyes.

In order to make such an abstract idea come to life, we need a living symbol well within the area of our understanding. Our minds can take hold of a graphic illustration of a spiritual principle at work in human experience. But that kind of an illustration is not easy to find. I had almost despaired of finding one that would fit our needs, until one day I met your good friend and mine, Sol Nemkov, for many years first violinist of the NBC orchestra. He said, "I have an interesting story for you. I don't know how you would relate it to your preaching, but you will, so I will tell it to you for what it may be worth." Then, as if in answer to my prayer, he unfolded a story that perfectly illustrates the rather abstract idea of the indwelling of God's creative spirit in the soul of man.

176

The story I would use this morning makes the idea of spiritual indwelling come alive in a modern context. It points out that such an indwelling is a mixture of high privilege and real responsibility, self-mastery and self-dedication.

In this story that seems made to order for our purpose we have a miracle of our time, a story of imagination, courage, artistic sensitivity, and a practical faith. It shows the power of a great personality on the lives of men even when the physical being may be removed by circumstance. It is so real and close to us that each one of us in our own way can enter into the human experience that is involved and feel it as our own.

Our story is about a great inspiration, a modern miracle of communication, and a man of creative genius. It tells the story of an orchestra that refused to die and of an artistic idea that gave it life. Some people have called it the miracle of Carnegie Hall.

Let us start at the beginning, with a man who is something of a miracle himself. You all know the name of David Sarnoff, an immigrant lad who came to this country with a great belief in its possibility for him and his obligation to it. He early became interested in wireless. One night years ago he was at work on his experiments when he picked up a crackling code message and first brought to the world the news of the sinking of the *Titanic*. That message made him instantly a great figure in radio telegraphy. He went on from that early experience to become a major figure in science and industry, one of the minor miracles of America, although he would be a major miracle anywhere else in the world.

David Sarnoff has been filled with a deep sense of gratitude to the nation that made it possible for him to do so much with his life. He appreciated the benefits of the life he had found here, and he was mature enough to know that every privilege carries with it a responsibility. Not only was he a man of science and industry, but also he was and is a patron of the arts. He is a lover of great music. When he thought of his obligation to the country that had given him such great opportunities, he quite naturally thought in terms of a gift of undying beauty.

More than a generation ago, Mr. Sarnoff knew that one of the greatest conductors of symphonic music had just retired. With artistic imagination and a keen sense of human values, Mr. Sarnoff offered Mr. Toscanini an opportunity to create a great new orchestra, made to his own dimensions, and bringing together the finest artistic talent available. This orchestra was to fulfill an artist's dream and a cultural need in America. Mr. Toscanini responded. For seventeen years that orchestra lived as a symbol of the ability of American culture to gather together the best of the world's heritage and make it live with a new sense of beauty and meaning.

This orchestra became a living symbol of music at its best. While it upheld the standard of musical perfection, it also gave free rein to the artist's imaginative interpretation. There the great mind of a great maestro used the artistic ability of a hundred fine musicians to recapture and express again the inspiration of those musical creators of the past and the present whose souls come alive in their music. Here the finest in symphonic music would receive the finest interpretation for the benefit of all listening America.

All of us have heard that great orchestra. It became a well-loved part of Sunday afternoon. During years of hardship and stress it emphasized again that there was beauty and goodness at the core of man's nature. We have felt a strange kinship with that orchestra for we felt that somehow it was fulfilling a deep need of our souls. For seventeen years this orchestra brought great glory to the field of symphonic music and great music to the lives of unnumbered Americans.

In the past there have been great orchestras, in our own and other countries. But there has never been any orchestra quite like this in its origin, its contribution, and its at-one-ness with the cultural needs and aspirations of a great and vigorous people. It fulfilled a unique function. It was an orchestra that in its very nature was created to give expression to an idea of musical perfection in the life of an old man who refused to be old, and with his concept of musical interpretation sought to bring to life again a quality of musical genius that seemed to have died. His ideal of perfection was a stern master. Often he drove the men of his orchestra mercilessly, and they gloried in it. He fulfilled through them the demands of a great discipline, the creative compulsion of the artistic genius.

Through those seventeen years we steeped our souls in that great privilege, and then, suddenly, we became aware of the tragic fact that it was no more. That grand old man of music, at eighty-seven, felt entitled to lay down his baton. That April night as he concluded the chords of the Overture to *Die Meistersinger,* laid down his baton, and walked from the podium, everyone realized that something noble in the life of American music had come to an end. Some even felt that the orchestra without its maestro ceased to have significance. Shortly thereafter the members of the orchestra received notice that their services would no longer be needed. There was nothing strange about this from the practical point of view. Those of us who had listened to that orchestra for seventeen years had been willing to accept all of the privileges and accept none of the responsibilities. I know, for I listened to it hundreds of times and never once wrote to thank the organization that made it possible. You and millions like you were as remiss as I had been. We might try to excuse ourselves by feeling that this program was above and beyond the demands of commercial interest. We knew that popular programs were sustained by popular demand, but this orchestra seemed to be so completely in a class by itself that we did not want to confuse it with other types of entertainment, even to recognizing its need for support in the thought and interest of an appreciative people. We did not thank the radio stations that gave the time. We did not thank the organization that assumed the financial obligations. We did not indicate to anyone that what had been done for us was not only appreciated but highly valued. We took it for granted as we do many of the blessings of American life. Those who rated the orchestra on the basis of the response of the listening public felt there was no justification for its continued existence. So, although it was a magnificent musical body, there was no place for it in America after its leader retired.

This decision came as a shock to the music lovers of America, and even more so to those men who had bound up their lives so closely with the orchestra. But the shock came too late for the music lovers of the nation to respond. The decision had been made.

The men of the orchestra, however, felt that in a real sense they were a living part of the soul of Toscanini. Through their years of intimate and fruitful association they had become mastered by his interpretive genius. They felt they had something priceless within themselves. Part of his very soul lived on in them. They had been the instruments through which that soul found expression. Was all that to come to an end? Even though they were dejected in spirit, they could not make themselves feel that this was the final answer. Although they were disheartened, there was a music in their souls that responded to the interpretive genius that had been built into the very structure of their lives. The image and thought of the great maestro stood always before them.

Then some of the musicians met together and said in effect, "This cannot be the end of us." They called together the other members of the orchestra and talked the matter over. Then one day they sat down and voted themselves back into life. It was a precarious life. They had no treasury. When they were offered a European tour, they had to refuse, for they did not have enough money to get themselves aboard the boat.

To prove to themselves and others the power of the indwelling spirit of their maestro, they made some recordings with only his spiritual presence to conduct them. Already these records have become collectors' items. As they rehearsed, they felt themselves guided by a spirit of musical interpretation that had mastered their lives. This musical body without a leader in the flesh remained under the control of the spirit of a man who had come to play so important a part in their artistic life that they would never be able to play as if his inspiration was not real to them. For to them Toscanini had become something more than a man. He had become a tradition, an ideal of musical perfection. His spirit lived on in them.

This revived orchestra decided on a daring venture to prove to the world that it was not dead. The members decided to do something that had never been done before in all the history of symphonic music. Although they did not have enough money in their treasury to make a down payment on Carnegie Hall, they pooled their private resources and hired it. They reserved a night and started to practice in earnest. They found that somehow deep within themselves there had been planted a musical responsiveness to the great conductor that would not die. Almost innately and unconsciously his interpretations lived on in them in the music they had done together.

When the night of the concert came, Carnegie Hall was filled. There was mixed doubt and fear and hope. Surely it was a moment of musical triumph as an orchestra of a hundred men played magnificently and with stirring perfection—and all without a leader. At least, that was what the newspapers said. There was no leader before them to wave a baton, but surely they had found a leadership that was at work in every fiber of their being. They responded. As a great group of creative artists can respond, they surpassed the expectations of those who listened, and almost instantly the musical world realized that something significant had happened. These men of the orchestra had refused to let something great within themselves die. What seemed an end was really a new beginning. When they sat down to practice, they could close their eyes and see Toscanini. In concert his living spirit stood before them. The spirit of the master had become a part of their lives.

I do not need to amplify this story to make you see how this brings to life the idea of the indwelling of the spirit of God in the lives of men. The inspiration of a great idea can stimulate life to seemingly impossible heights of achievement. After the death of Jesus, the disciples were dejected, defeated, and ready to disperse. Then they found the reality of the spirit that dwelt among them, and their lives were changed. They set out with courage and undying inspiration to change the world. They had found the power of a spiritual ideal that would not die. These men of the early church became living instruments to transmit the idea of a triumphant way of life to a world filled with bitterness, sin, and strife.

But lest we be misled, we must know two things about this indwelling spirit. It brings to life rich privileges and real responsibilities. As with the NBC orchestra, we are often willing to accept the privileges but are loath to accept the responsibilities that go with it. Who knows but that we might still be spending our Sunday afternoons listening to great music if a few millions of persons in the course of seventeen years had accepted the small responsibility of saying, "Thank you." Who knows but that this musical organization could have continued to live if a million people who loved great music in the Toscanini tradition had made their thanks explicit by backing their words of appreciation with the coin of the realm.

The privileges of life sooner or later have commensurate responsibilities and the mature person is the one who is aware of the fact and acts accordingly. The values of the religious life are rich in meaning and bring to life a quality of inner resources to deal with the ultimate issues of human experience. But those benefits require also a discipline of life, a preparation of mind and emotions that can make the benefits possible. The disciples of Jesus found life's meaning in complete devotion to the ideal of life bequeathed to them by their Master. The followers of Toscanini and the lovers of great music find a fulfillment of a cultural possibility in a willingness to accept the belief that something great in the world of music must not be allowed to die.

You and I, in our own lives, begin to realize our possibilities for great living when we learn the healthy balance that comes when privileges and responsibilities are both accepted with honesty, and the quality of living is determined by the indwelling of that spirit of God that demands from us the fullest realization of our own undying spiritual nature.